THE RANGE OF COMMITMENT

The Range of Commitment

ESSAYS OF A CONSERVATIVE LIBERAL

Justus George Lawler

THE BRUCE PUBLISHING COMPANY / Milwaukee

Library of Congress Catalog Card Number: 68–55280

Copyright © 1969 JUSTUS GEORGE LAWLER
MADE IN THE UNITED STATES OF AMERICA

FOR TOMMY AND GEORGIE

FOREWORD

When one is writing the introduction to a book such as this, all the conventions suggest a modest disclaimer of interest in its fate. The tone of the rhetoric should imply diffidence, even disdain about the whole effort: an obsequious editor venally foisted the project on a hesitant author. It's a standard ploy. Friends of the author can criticize the book without criticizing him; the author himself can plead as motive charity toward his publisher rather than self-service toward himself, and everybody can rejoice in his intellectual purity—except of course the crass publisher, who doesn't matter anyway.

But it won't wash. Nobody twists an author's arm to produce something like the present collection. The author is responsible for it entirely, and in the present case has no intention of evading that responsibility. He is, moreover, grateful to what he would like to think of as a discerning publisher and editor for sponsoring the work.

Some of the essays that make up this book were written as far back as the years before Vatican II, and others as recently as 1968. Where necessary they have been amended slightly with regard to factual matters, but the basic position assumed, regardless of how dated it might now appear to some, has not been changed. Nor do I see any reason that it should be. In one or two cases I would say things quite differently while maintaining nevertheless my original orientation, as in the pieces on priesthood and episcopate; the former particularly strikes me as much too rigorously schematized, too rigid, too doctrinaire. But the fundamental stance I would not shift: as long as we have institutions—and we shall have them as long as man lives in society—we shall have order, hierarchy, distinction of roles and separation of functions. The present trend toward blurring everything into one indistinguishable mass, however flattering to the ambitious or the rootless, can only be regarded as signifying how transitional a state we are in. Whether we call bishops or popes chief clerks, presiding officers, or chairmen of the board, matters not at all. What matters is that government and authority exist and be administered by someone, regardless of title.

Both of the essays on priesthood and episcopacy should be read in the light of the remarks on collegiality elsewhere in this book and of other comments on the office of the layman, particularly those in *The Catholic Dimension in Higher Education*. In view of the bishops' abdication of collegiality when faced by *Humanae vitae*, I would probably now be less sanguine about the American hierarchy than I was nearly a decade ago. But as Newman's Tractarian remnant affirmed in a similar case of episcopal betrayal, ultimately we don't put our trust in the bishops, we put it in the whole Church.

It is the whole Church which has been affronted by *Humanae vitae*, and since the arguments on which it based its negative conclusions regarding contraception are precisely those controverted in the treatment of that issue here, far from feeling that this particular piece ought to be modified or withdrawn, I think it ought to be all the more strongly endorsed. For what is needed in the present critical moment is not silence or lament or rebellion, but a renewal of the philosophical and theological struggle which everybody outside of Rome believed had been won some years back. The natural law issue remains the crux of that struggle.

As every Chartreuse-drinking layman can attest, bishops and popes as we now know them will pass, the Church will remain. That is the meaning of this book. It is a book which affirms the continuing need for the institutional, and which proclaims that as institutional, it must change and be changed. That is the meaning of conservative liberalism.

It remains only to thank the various publications where these essays first appeared. "Theology and the Uses of History": *Continuum* and *New Theology V*. "The Bishops as Teachers": *Commonweal*. "Priests in the World": *Commonweal*. "Charles Davis: The Glamour of Dissent": *Commonweal*, *Continuum*, and *The Christian Century*. "Antisemitism and Theological Arrogance": *Herder Correspondence* and *Continuum*. "Contraception and Natural Law": *Contraception and Holiness*, *New Blackfriars*, and *Continuum*. "Marxism as Propaedeutic": *Continuum*. "In Defense

of the Catholic University": *Continuum* and *The Catholic Mind.*
"Aid to Catholic Schools": *Commonweal.* "The Future of Belief
Debate": *The Critic* and *New Theology VI.* "Towards a Theology
of Animals": *The Anglican Theological Review, Jubilee,* and
Continuum. "Diction as Morality": *Continuum.* "Matter Ec-
clesia": *Continuum.*

This book closes too long a phase beginning with my first published article in *America* in 1944, and extending to 1969: twenty-
five years of concern with affairs Catholic.

> At last he rose, and twitched his mantle blue:
> Tomorrow to fresh woods, and pastures new.

JUSTUS GEORGE LAWLER

CONTENTS

I

THEOLOGY AND THE
USES OF HISTORY

In the context of one of the studies to appear later in this book, "Priests in the World," I had occasion to observe in *Commonweal* at the time of the article's original publication: "Pluck 'religionless religion' and what is left is a new apologetic, very good, very necessary, but in the end very much a matter of apologetic, a heightening of terminology only."[1] There is little reason for revising this judgment, even though it is evident that God's ardent theological undertakers are seeking to invest their earlier rhetoric with some substantive values. This latter stems in part from the demands of the intellectual community for payment in hard cash on the inflationary vouchers which have been flooding the marketplace of religious speculation; it stems also, and more dangerously, from the mesmerizing effect the repetition of their own catch-phrases has had on the members of the death-of-God persuasion who are now driven either through psychological fixation or mere self-defense to reify their own jargon.

Nevertheless, no one questions — though E. L. Mascall in *The Secularization of Christianity*[2] comes perilously close to doing so — that the hydra-headed phenomenon known variously or collectively as religionless religion, secularization, God is dead, etc., constitutes a portentous sign of the times, the sources of which, as diverse as the manifestations, may be set forth serially as follows. There is, first of all, the response — strongly though not exclusively German — to the failure of the churches to withstand

---

[1] *Commonweal* (June 18, 1965).
[2] New York, 1966; cf. my review, *Herder Correspondence Book Supplement* (March, 1966).

1

the corrosive force of fascism and nationalism: the churches having been too other-worldly in the past seek now to rectify the old failings, sometimes by a quasi-identification with the city of man. Parallel to this sociological reaction is the specifically religious rebound from the total negation of natural theology in Barth to the affirmation of the natural — meaning the secular — as the sole basis for theologizing: or not theologizing. There is, third, the evident failure of traditional language and symbols meaningfully to express the presence of God among contemporary men; and on the one hand the consequent search for his presence outside of the realm ordinarily denominated "the sacred," and on the other hand, the conclusion that what cannot be adequately symbolized may not exist. Fourth, there is the growing sense of the importance of the temporal and contingent in a religion, Christianity, which is so decisively history-centered and act-centered. Fifth, there is the greater awareness of the selfness of man, of his unique spirithood — represented historically by the Romantic movement in all its facets — and the attendant disdain for the seemingly static categories enshrined in much of the theology of the West. Derivative from this on a more superficial plane is the assumption that the authentic utterance of any man, whether atheist or not, is a more deeply religious act, because more deeply human, than the feigned prayer or the sacramental confection of the professed believer. And, finally, there is modern man's experienced mastery of the universe — of which Teilhard is the Christian spokesman — and the recognition that this mastery is the fulfillment of man's destiny only when he envisions the "world" not as his enemy but as his co-conspirator.

All of these currents, radical, reactionary, liberal, evolutionary, have generated their own variants or composites of the central stream and their own enlargements of orthodoxy or extensions of heresy. The thrust of the larger drift is provided by the not very novel insight that all words used of God are inadequate and that whatever words man uses must come from his own self-appropriation of the absolute in his own temporal experience. The intellectual morass into which some of these channels have flowed arises from the failure to realize that precisely because man does shape his own destiny, does control his own evolution, not every manifestation of the age is by the fact of its mere appearance therefore ratified as good. Here the issue is to determine a standard relevant to the temporal order once the trans-temporal has been implicitly cancelled out. The world cannot be moved without a fulcrum, and traditionally it has seemed self-evident that that fulcrum cannot be the world itself.

It is this canonization of the exclusively temporal and this attendant exclusion of any prophetic surety in judging the world which has been the butt of most orthodox Christian criticism of the religionless-religion current. This is a tenable line of criticism, but it is obviously more defensive than offensive, and one is therefore entitled to search out a much more fundamental criticism of those various new theologians whose implicit strategy seems to be the wholesale evacuation of the Christian position. A radically more fundamental criticism must necessarily concern itself not with theology and theologian but with humanism and man. And it is the contention here that such aberrations as the death-of-God theology can flourish only because of the exaggerated professionalism, the intense inbreeding, and the morbidly heightened theological consciousness of those many theologians who, having given themselves over to "the study of divine things," can glimpse human realities only in their most exaggerated and elephantine forms, and even then can glimpse them only "under the aspect of" themselves not as men but as theologians. The point of departure for the critique will not be the jets of paraphraseable or translatable thought that occasionally burst forth from the bogs of Emory University or Colgate Divinity School, but some observations of thoroughly orthodox religious scholars at Notre Dame's conference on the theological issues of Vatican II.

What is most striking about these various papers is their almost studied avoidance of any theological reflection as such; the great mass of the statements presented was concerned with assessments of the condition of modern man, with much shorthand sociology, history, artistic and literary opining — all embraced as indicators of the direction in which theology must go in the future. It is commendable that theologians should take into account the signs of the times; they simply must do so if they are to avoid exiling themselves to the deserts of irrelevance. But they must make such an accounting as theologians who are first of all men and who are therefore, and secondly, wary of the easy ascription of humane values to every human activity. One must therefore pause at Fr. Walter Burghardt's maintaining:

This man committed to Nothing is a frightening phenomenon of our time. It is an attitude towards reality that stems from at least four sources: (1) a creeping collectivism, where "the people" suppresses the individual; (2) a growing dehumanization, symbolized by Dachau, the mushroom cloud, and the shelter doorway; (3) an increasing automation, represented by the IBM card; (4) the apparent failure of organized religion to redeem the world. In this attitude, man's dignity and his hope lie in his ability to confront, with courage and indeed with joy, a life and a reality that is senseless, useless, absurd. Man is alone, isolated, a stranger to himself, to the world, to God. The hell of Sartre — hell is other people — has given place to the hell of Bergman — hell is being alone.

This affirmation of Nothing leaps out at you from the creative arts: from the painting of a Pollock, through the music of a Cage, to the poetry of Kazantzakis. It is spendidly summed up by Samuel Beckett: two times anything equals zero.[3]

Fr. Burghardt is a careful and large-minded thinker, but nonetheless one cannot help wondering what we really do know either about man of the past or of the present that would justify the claim that man as here defined is a "phenomenon of our time." Our awareness of creeping collectivism may be more intense than was thirteenth-century man's awareness of what might well have been — and historically, *contra* Christopher Dawson, looks very much like — an even more monstrous collectivism, simply because contemporary man can articulate what could only take the form of a suppressed grunt of outrage for men of past ages. Perhaps our awareness of such evils is greater only because man and his institutions in our time have reached so much higher a plane of humanism. And so too with each of the other "frightening phenomena of our time": why not parallel them with the dehumanization of the perennial pogroms of Christian Europe, with the Albigensian crusades, with the castles barred against the plague-stricken outside the walls, and so on? But the point is not to counter any of Fr. Burghardt's assertions with other perhaps equally questionable assertions, but simply to indicate that historical judgments such as his are not demonstrably well-

---

[3] *Vatican II: An Interfaith Appraisal* (Notre Dame, 1966), p. 638.

founded and that therefore a theology based on them may be a chimera.

What Fr. Burghardt has given us — as the Quaker saying goes — tastes of the pipes. Christians of every denomination have been inundated by it before in innumerable articles and programs of study devoted to ferreting out Christ-figures and Adamic-types in all the English novels from Melville to Faulkner. It is the rare theologian — one thinks of William Lynch — who is so conversant with the contemporary arts that he can make religious sense out of them. More often than not he employs them as proof-texts for his own up-to-dateness (clerics in Harry Truman sport shirts: *that* up-to-date), as pegs to hang a thesis on (William Hamilton mis-quoting Stevens' "Sunday Morning") or as occasions for flying headers into *Kulturgeschichte* (Godot or Willy Loman envisioned as archetypes of contemporary man: *that* contemporary). In the latter instance, that sociologists or students of the behavioral sciences may view such heavily freighted symbolic fictions merely as the creations of cultural sports — in the strict biological sense — merely as expressions of the most involute subgroups, is usually ignored.

This is merely by way of noting (for the time being) that it is always desirable to keep one's categories clean; highly refined specialists like theologians ought to take measure only of what is actually known by those other highly refined specialists whose field of interest is man's present condition, his communities, his sense of the temporal, etc. This, of course, implies that all groups of specialists must rely primarily on their fundamental human experience (of which more shortly) and secondarily on their pro-fessional acquisitions. The fusion of religious commitment with amateur literary or sociological extrapolation does little to serve either theology or the citizen of the secular city. The latter, to the degree he can be shown to exist, will be better aided by theological speculation as such — undertaken in the light of the fundamental human experience — and less by spinning religio-cultural generali-ties out of Fellini and Camus.

The enormities which so much theology today easily assimilates can be explained only as the result of the atrophy of the human experience itself and the consequent attempt to com-pensate, necessarily at second hand, for this withering up of spirit by a junket through the arts in search of the lost innocence. Theology today — and this is true of most specialized disciplines save those that are directly rooted in the experience of being — is in a state with regard to the secular city comparable to the state of the whole literate culture vis à vis the mass of men in the thirteenth century. One shudders at the thought of what we might have if St. Thomas had devoted himself to being up on Guillaume de Lorris or — more up-to-date and secular — Guido Cavalcanti, rather than to experiencing the reality and elaborating the meaning embodied in the insight that "the intellect in the act of intellecting proceeds into infinity." And this, because the experience this insight represents is what defines man as man, whether he be the man of the dark ages or the man of the city of Nothing.

"It is the function of theology to be a servant," Fr. Burghardt notes. "In our time this demands service on three levels: the City of God, the City of Man, and what I can only call the No-City."[4] One needn't question again: why "in our time"? Yet even after acknowledging the large truth in his formulation, one must inquire precisely how theology fulfills this ancillary function. The danger of enlisting theology in the service of "our time" is that theology may be made irrelevant to itself, that is, to its task of plumbing the infinite. This is all the more likely when one considers the plasticity, the vagueness and imprecision that attach to all serious efforts at precisioning with any kind of rigor the characteristic notes of our time. Given the fact that no theologian has any right to trust his private intuitings about the nature of this historical epoch, given the added fact that there is neither unanimity nor even a loose consensus among culture historians or social scientists about that nature, and given the final fact that there is no reason yet to assume contemporary man's radical dissociation from man of the past — the experience of the trans-finite is the single criterion and its application here would not confirm such dissociation — one can be optimistic about the future of theology only to the degree that theology is true to itself and its basic datum.

It could not unprofitably be borne in mind that the one mas-

---

4 *Ibid.*

sive theological achievement, though still in process, of a North American Catholic scholar stems not from any urgent, and however otherwise laudable, need for assuaging the anxieties of somebody's paradigm of the "man of our time," but from the exigencies of theological science as such. One will look in vain in the work of Bernard Lonergan for a theology inspired by the ad hoc dredgings of the present moment of history; and precisely because Lonergan's theology is to that degree "self-serving," precisely because it is theology, it continues to be of service and to speak to the needs of the contemporary world. The Christian community has been surfeited with skeletal theologies clumsily coopted to this or that sociological conception, this or that literary school, this or that psychological or political theory: theologies which stand as objects of amusement or bewilderment to the practitioners or promotors of those various other disciplines and programs.

If it is rejoined that theology to be self-serving must both serve the world and draw upon the world's services in turn, the answer can only be, of course. Of course, all history is salvation history in a sense, but the determination of what in "salvation history in a sense" is truly salvific can only be made by the students of "salvation history without qualification." And if it is further rejoined that whatever we know of God we know by his acts in history, the answer must again be, of course — with the proviso now, that while man in history can only know of God's acts, the knowledge of these acts does lead to or is, a trans-historical experience. And it is primarily in reflection upon this experience that the theologian fulfills his mission.

Theologians ought to make no more of history than their inevitable immersion in it demands. That they do make so much more of it results mainly — among other things — from the separation of their understanding of God's acts from the trans-historical experience such understanding should have fostered, but did not. Without moorings in the transcendental experience, without the experience that the light one sees is the light by which one sees, their theology is irrelevant to itself and irrelevant to man who seeks such an experience as the natural end of his earthly being. In their search for this vanishing relevance, the theologians are more and more driven directly to relate their speculations to the immediate condition of man; they study his rootlessness, his anomie, and proffer their solutions — tricked out in whatever sociological categories may be current — from out of their compendia of religious data.

It is a truism that man comes to know himself only in the act of knowing another, and that he comes to know himself most fully in knowing, however inchoately, the being of God. But many theologians, rather than looking at this "other" — which implies a genuine alterity — look only at themselves; caught in endless mental ipsation, what they give to the living man is not the fruit of humane experience, but only the mirror image of their own insecurity, reinforced usually by the mirror images of other sciences, that is, only the fabrication known as "God is Dead." But this god, when stripped of his splendid verbal trappings, is only an abstraction of inhumane man; he is what Wallace Stevens called "the total man of glubbal glub"[5] — which is merely to say this god reveals himself in the language of Altizer and Hamilton.

Theologians no more than any others ought not to view themselves as divorced from the spirit of the times, from the flux of the present, and ought not therefore to feel they must compensate for their imagined divorce by an artificial and self-conscious immersion of their theology in what they take to be the dominant social, political, and cultural traits of the age. A little more confidence in themselves as men in history — that is, as beings defined as "vocations to the infinite" — would make them better theologians. Given their inescapable human disposition, they would do better to theologize out of the driving insights — born of the transcendental experience — into their own science and not out of their necessarily secondhand grasp of the materials of other equally specialized fields. They would above all be better off as men and as theologians if they ceased conning the arts for types or symbols of "the human condition" and "the existential situation," and let themselves be open to the esthetic experience itself. Our secularized theologians are like the caricature of Goethe making love with pad and pen in hand to immortalize his raptures. This is the "other" seen not as "other" but as a machine for poeticizing — or theologizing. The kind of hybrid vision to which

[5] "Chocura to Its Neighbor."

this style of "doing" theology — as the new barbarism terms it — lends itself is apparent in some comments of Dr. Albert Outler, who shared Fr. Burghardt's platform at Notre Dame: "Now the reality of God becomes the central issue once more — and new patterns of inquiry in religious epistemology, religious anthropology, religious metaphysics, ontology and theology proper are the obvious tasks of the new generation who aim to convince men of the reality of God (of his presence and grace) in a world come of age and gone to pot."[6] Bonhoeffer cum Spengler cum theodicy: the religious sentiments can be no more laudable than the historical judgments are incredible.

But not all the voices raised at Notre Dame harmonized with such a rendition of the song of the earth. Fr. John Meyendorff, author of two important works on Gregory Palamas, in a few short paragraphs both broached the unchanging theological issue of our and all preceding times and also scored the current preoccupation with ministering to the needs of some contemporary image of man:

The Orthodox Church has committed itself, in the late Middle Ages, to affirming that God is absolutely and totally unknown in his essence, that no human faculty, not even the "beatific vision," is able to grasp the essence of God. Knowledge of God is possible only inasmuch as the living God manifests himself in the free acts of this love toward man. Between the honest agnostic and the Christian there is therefore this capital point of agreement: God is unknown to the human mind, and their dialogue consists in the responsibility of the Christian to show what is Divine Life, Divine Love, and where and how they are being met.

So, if we Orthodox join our Catholic brethren in facing the modern agnostic man, we are also led immediately in the discussion between the Palamite and the Thomist on the issue of the knowledge of God, on the making of the "spiritual senses," which are, according to the Fathers, our means of contact with the Living God; and whose existence we cannot prove to the atheist, nor even prove to ourselves, but whose reality we experience in the Church of God, as those things which, Paul said, "are prepared by God for those who love Him."

And if the knowledge of God is finally the very content of the Christian faith, and if this knowledge can be shown and accepted only in the total freedom of the human person answering with love to God's love, is the Roman Church always right in its traditional preoccupation — which is still certainly not totally absent in the

---

[6] Vatican II: An Interfaith Appraisal, p. 622.

Vatican II decisions — to administer human society, to find solutions to all human problems, to guide, to feed, to advise, to rule and to direct instead of *showing*?[7]

There is much here to which one might take exception: it is too negative, and it assumes a gap between the Palamite and the Thomist which is largely nonexistent. But it does raise the theological question, the question of plumbing the depths of the unknown God; the question of today as of yesterday as of the future. Unquestionably theology is made in history as God is known *somehow* in history; and the human ambiance affects theologians no less than other men. But we know what little we do know of contemporary history only by indirection, and the theologian contributes in his own unique way to that knowledge not by gleaning the sociological data but by his necessarily historically conditioned and unselfconscious theologizing on the fundamental experience of being, and on the religious experience of God's presence to man in the Church. The theologian *is* a man in history; he finds himself there, he does not put himself there. And it is by being true to the demands of his own science, by making good theology, that he makes also his own contribution both to the spirit of the historical epoch and to man's understanding of it.

What the Palamite would call "the making of the spiritual senses," the Thomist would call the experiencing of the transcendent, an experience which though disfigured in much traditional Christian and even Thomistic thinking is utterly obscured by the theologies of the death of God. It is a stereotype of such modish trends that "the presence of God takes the form of a simultaneous and terrifying absence of God." The statement is by Eugene Fontinell[8] and parallels the following similar sentiment from an otherwise excellent book by Michael Novak: "If, occasionally, I raise my heart in prayer, it is to no God I can see, or hear, or feel."[9] In both cases we have the utterance of a commonplace — though Novak's ambiguity is heavier by his use of "feel" which is both a transitive and intransitive verb — explicitly endorsed by a whole tradition from Dionysius on through the greatest medieval commentary on *The Divine Names* (Aquinas meeting Palamas); in

[7] *Ibid.*, pp. 615–616.
[8] *Cross Currents* (Winter, 1966).
[9] *Belief and Unbelief* (New York, 1965), preface.

fact, explicitly endorsed by virtually every Christian thinker, and implicitly by the great God-haters such as Blake, Nietzsche, and Jeffers. But as understood by the radical theologians this commonplace is distorted to mean the total lack of any awareness of God's presence.

But traditionally even God as Absence is a knowledge, a way of knowing by not-knowing, a knowledge of the contours of what will go into a vessel from the vacuities, the emptinesses of the vessel which God has elected to fill. But this is a longing for the infinite, and as such a negative knowledge. The positive aspect is an experience of God precisely as presence, as a presence which is a fulfillment rather than an emptiness seeking to be fulfilled. Obviously the two are aspects of the same reality, for the nearer men draw to God the farther he is from them and the greater is their longing and their fulfillment. Nor does it diminish the positive character of this sense of God as present that it can only be described in negative terms, as *nada*; or, more simply put, as the subjunctive to the indicative — which is the modal relationship of any expression of the experience of spirit, whether through a person, a poem, or a truth.

There are two aspects of this positive presence of God to man. The first, finely underlined by Bernard Lonergan, is an explicitation of the maxim central to Augustine, Aquinas, Pascal, and Newman that we would not seek God if we did not somehow possess him. The other is a "knowledge" which, though derivative of the preceding notion of "spirit as inquiry," "existential exigency," "vocation to the infinite," or, even "obediential potency," has a greater richness to it. This is the knowledge no less unformulatable, no less inenarrable than any other knowledge of God, yet nonetheless and precisely because of its very ineffableness, a true and deep knowledge. This is the gradual shaping out — through a greater and greater frequency of recurrence of the experience of being — of one's sense of the infinite. It is not so much a question of an accumulation which results in an intensifying of the experience itself as it is of an accumulation which keeps adding new facets to the polygon of understanding as it seeks to embrace and be embraced by the infinite circle of mystery. And it is this shaping out — obviously never clearly, never definitively — this "habitus" of the transcendental experience, which alone when joined to theological

competence can account for the insights of a Rahner, a de Lubac, a
von Balthasar — though the latter would perhaps regret its present formulation.[10] Not the most highly refined rational skills,
however indispensable, can explain the fecundity of the elaboration of the Christian message evidenced in the writings of theologians such as these.

Parenthetically it should be noted that it is this understanding
of the transcendental experience which is at the core of what is
rightly regarded as the most significant attainment of truly contemporary and therefore truly traditional Catholic thought. It is
the *point de départ* of Maréchal, the *Geist in Welt* of Rahner,
the *surnaturel* of de Lubac, the *Metaphysik* of Coreth, the *Insight*
of Lonergan — and one could add, the basis of Novak's application of the latter in *Belief and Unbelief*, and of Boros' application
of Blondel in *The Mystery of Death*.

Yet it is no mere cavil — rather it is the whole point of the
earlier discussion above — to emphasize the fact that, that this
"new" understanding should be viewed as so significant an attainment can only strike the poet and the artist, that is to say, man at
his best, as the astonishing proof of how detached from the experience of being is most philosophy of religion. Such are the pitfalls of the institutionalization and professionalization of intellectual enterprises, including above all theology as the subject of
churchmen, that that experience which is most immediate to man
in his authenticity should reappear tardily as a novel discovery
to academic thinkers. There is more to it than this, of course,
for it is a question for the religious philosopher of not merely
being aware of the undistilled experience but of validating as
discursively as possible its reality and articulating as fully as possible its implications; and for the theologian as such, it is a question of distinguishing between what in the natural order is the
element of *chance*, adventitiousness, in the encounter with being
and what in the supernatural order is the absolute *gratuity* of
God's addressing his Word to man in the Church. Nevertheless
one cannot but be put in mind, when reading even the writings of
the transcendental Thomists of someone who came to realize the
meaning of love only after researching, say, Fromm and Freud.

---

[10] Cf. *Glaubhaft Ist nur Liebe* (Einsiedeln, 1963), chapter 2.

There is no evading "natural" theology and this transcendental experience which grounds it. If Barth in reaction to pietism feared the religious experience, so much the worse for Barth; theology is not politics and the fact that a theologian is a powerful intellectual force provides no guaranteed mandate for his views.[11] It is this transcendental experience alone which preserves religious experience from anthropomorphism, whether the anthropomorphism of "Caliban upon Setebos," or the more refined though identical anthropomorphism of pop theologians who compose out of their own impenetrability and imperviousness the concept of God as the cosmic mortician who can only affect us after we are dead — if then. Yet such composition is in no way surprising: religious philosophers who never go beyond the conceptual, who traffic only in concepts, however sophisticated these may be, must conclude, when faced by their inevitable failure to conceptualize Being, that there is no Being at all.

And that is why the death-of-God theology is rightly denominated "pop." Pop art was the carefully tended nursling of neo-academic critics; it allowed them to appear as rebels against their own conventions and above all it allowed them to fulfill what they envision — indeed, what they get paid for and prove their *raison d'être* by — as the critic's highest function: *talk*. Since the pop painting was so negligible as to be almost non-existent as an artifact (Painting is dead!), all that really mattered to a truly contemporary critic was talk about, around, behind, and across the picture. Pop art made the critic more important than the artwork itself, even as pop theology makes the concepts of theologians more important than the being of God. (For tangential theological discourse going off aimlessly and telling us nothing about God but a great deal about himself and about his ideas and his feelings and his opinions one must heed the voice of Professor Altizer.)

Professor Altizer's colleague, William Hamilton, indulges when theologizing his belltristic inclinations, and mythicizes the religious revolution through which modern man is believed to be passing with the assertion that Oedipal theology is giving way to Orestes

---

[11] That Barth no longer regards the analogy of being as the work of antichrist is common knowledge. Cf. H. Bouillard, *Connaissance de Dieu* (Paris, 1967), chapter 4.

theology, and that the epoch of Hamlet religion is being sup-
planted by the epoch of Prospero religion. This is an exemplary
heuristic device. So let it be said instead that the revolt is *against*
the religious, establishmentarian priggishness of a Prince Hal and
is *for* the spontaneous, commoner's exuberance of a Falstaff. But
the watchword is "demythologize." And no poetic imagery should
blind us to the basic datum that monarch and fool are not distinguished rightly by their kingship or their buffoonery, but by
their humanness, a humanness which remains, throughout whatever alleged revolutions, radically defined as "openness to the
infinite." For this we must call upon the poet, not to put him to
work for us, but simply "to hear the word of the bard":

> The voice I hear this passing night was heard
>   In ancient days by emperor and clown:
> Perhaps the self-same song that found a path
>   Through the sad heart of Ruth, when, sick for home,
>   She stood in tears amid the alien corn.[12]

The present epoch of the eclipse of light will pass; it is already
a passing night, and Falstaff and Hal will be seen in the dawn for
what they truly are: the everyman who is Ruth in exile gleaning
what nurture she can for the journey home.

This is the tradition; this is man *with* a history. It may be ex-
punged from the anthologies of the theologians; it may be driven
out of academe. It cannot be annihilated in the human heart because it is what makes the heart human.

---

[12] Keats, "Ode to a Nightingale."

II

THE BISHOPS AS TEACHERS

The spirit of reform and renewal in the Church has obviously
been profoundly stimulated by the work of Vatican II. The atmosphere is considerably clearer now, with books appearing in all the
major languages on the renovation of our religious institutions,
than it was a decade and a half ago when so masterful a work as
Congar's *Vraie et fausse réforme* was withdrawn from circulation.
Since Catholicism is an incarnational faith which must at once
embrace the contingent multiplicity of history while remaining
faithful to its own inner spiritual unity, the difficulties in every
reform or renewal are the same as those encountered in any
human act. "How shall we know the dancer from the dance?"[1]
asked the poet; how shall we live the changeless principles in a
world of change? How shall we move in this world in harmonic
response to the choreography of the other world?

It is a question of maintaining a creative tension between the
two poles of reality. The first extreme to be avoided is that of
submitting blindly to the flux of change. One may be seduced
by the contingent either in conforming fully to it, or in reacting
so violently against it as to seek to repudiate the whole direction
of the present moment. Both are aspects of the same slavery.
One thinks in the first instance of the obsessive theme, running
through so many of Baron von Hügel's letters in René Marlé's
collection, *Au cœur de la crise moderniste*,[2] that the Church
might fail to gain recognition in the world of the twentieth-century
savant if it did not follow in the train of Abbé Loisy. In the
second instance, one thinks of the moderately liberal Pius IX

---

[1] Yeats, "Among School Children."
[2] Paris, 1960.

returning from exile in Gaeta to hurl anathemas at the nineteenth century.

In both illustrations I am oversimplifying, since these were men on whom a whole complexus of forces necessarily played; but the points to be made are, first, that blind submission to the data of the present moment or violent rebellion against them leads down the same path of sterility; and second, that it is not only in the Old Testament but in all of history that God moves through time and achieves his ends through vehicles that have all the blemishes of human nature in them. It is not surprising that the acts of the first Vatican Council are sometimes reminiscent of the reports in the *Congressional Record*, or that after the Council in order to force certain recalcitrant German bishops to make their public submission, the Roman authorities employed methods akin to those of a successful political machine.[3] Man lives in time and through temporal instruments his salvation comes.

The opposite extreme from this captivity by history is the attempt to flee into the world of absolute, changeless principles. Unfortunately, it is a flight which cannot succeed, since no human construct of ideas, no matter how lofty, can ever shed its temporal framework. In fact, the abstractionist, the victim of this angelism, often assumes that since the past is beyond the grasp of change and flux, it has about it some eternal and absolute value. The past for him becomes a substitute eternity — though the addicts of absolutism are also reaching out in their own way for the fugitive fusion of the one and the many. This is particularly the temptation of the metaphysician and theologian, both for the reasons I have just set forth and because the sciences they pursue do have about them a kind of suprahistorical aura. An example of this blind attachment to the petrifications of the past may be found in the pre-Vatican II argument that Church and State must be united because the State has an obligation as a kind of corporate person to worship the true God in the true way: in this case, the way of Catholicism. The notion was based largely on the ancient

---

[3] Cuthbert Butler, *The Vatican Council* (London, 1938), II, p. 187: "Rome was bringing silent pressure to bear [for acceptance of the decrees of Vatican I by Bishop Hefele] by withholding dispensations he applied for in marriage cases."

assumption — still evident in English law — that the State is the mystical body of the monarch; and thus an attack upon his people or his territories constituted an attack upon his person. In the homage paid to such an assumption by some ecclesiologists we have historical phenomena being wrought into the artifice of eternity.

The achievement of a balanced interpenetration of the two orders is the task of a lifetime, and of the lifetime of the human race. An historical figure — whose life and work bear on what I am about to say — that may be taken as a symbol of this merging of contingent realities with changeless principles is Cardinal Manning. One may sympathize, for example, with Newman's disdain for the teetotaler crusades which Manning so ardently backed, but one must acknowledge the truth of Newman's words describing his own career as that of one who lived "out of the world." And though there is in Manning much which is repugnant, so that he emerges not only from Strachey's portrait but from Purcell's and Leslie's also, as ruthlessly dedicated to the cause of the moment, it is obvious in the light of history that the causes he embraced were among the most important practical social issues of his day, and that he brought to them religious insights of the first order. Newman's life, as he himself saw it, was a unified evolutionary process, it was a development of doctrine from the time of his childhood conversion onwards. Manning's career, on the other hand, was compounded of frequent reversals of position dictated by changing events, and it had therefore an innate dialectical character about it.

One of the most striking of these reversals took place during the years following the Vatican Council. From fervent infallibilist, from the "majority whip" of Pius IX at the Council, Manning became in his later years highly suspicious of what he began to regard as the exorbitance of Rome. It was never a case of even faintly repudiating the doctrine of the Council, but rather of recognizing — what he could not see, however evident it may have been to other English bishops in 1870 — that the constitution on papal primacy had consequences in the practical order that tended to minimize the authority of the bishops. The result of this denigration of the bishop's authority, said Manning, was a "Catholic presbyterianism," which reduced the episcopal college to "only the Pope's vicariate."[4] That this encroachment on the episcopal office in the jurisdictional area derived in part from the incompleteness of the decrees of Vatican I, though true, was not very relevant to the actual situation subsequent to their proclamation. That the Council implicitly envisaged the Pope as a bishop "writ large," and did not view the local bishop as a lesser pope was generally lost sight of during the following fifty years: up, in fact, until the period of Rerum Ecclesiae of Pius XI (1926).

However, before discussing in detail these gradually developing correctives to the "papalism" of the post-Vatican I period, and their possible effect on American Catholicism, I would like to make some general remarks on what I had hoped to see result from the Second Vatican Council and its aftermath with regard to the bishops. What is expected from the Council and subsequent Bishops' Synods are primarily radical changes in the Church's organizational structure which are required by the demands of the present or by a renewed sense of tradition. Certainly one awaits few definitions of doctrine in the strict sense and fewer efforts at absolutist moral pronouncements; and one would expect whatever definitions may eventuate to be concerned with questions of the greatest present urgency. The intellectual heirs of Veuillot and William George Ward — the National Review-Triumph axis — are still active and still pressing for pronouncements on a multitude of questions. To these twentieth-century successors of the ultramontanists, one can only say with Newman: "When has definition of doctrine de fide been a luxury of devotion and not a stern, painful necessity?"[5]

In this general context one may, for example, express regret at the insistence with which certain authors call for a decision from the magisterium on such matters as monogenism or contraception. As to the first, it is not an issue over which the Catholic community is presently exercised, though its easy ventilation in the diocesan press may arouse an artificial interest in it and thus precipitate an otherwise patently inopportune decision. Anthropology and paleontology are still infant sciences, and they have not yet

---

[4] Shane Leslie, Henry Edward Manning (New York, 1921), p. 295.

[5] Wilfrid Ward, Life of John Henry Cardinal Newman (London, 1912), II 288.

been able to come up with anything capable of exerting a sufficiently strong impact on the virtually universal teaching of theologians and the injunctions of the Holy See to bring about even
a tentative exploration of the possible religious implications of
polygenism. Perhaps in two or three centuries a positive knowledge of the origin of man will have been elaborated and this
scientific elaboration may induce the theologians to re-examine
under such new stimulus the sources of their doctrinal teaching.
The possibility of intellectual beings on other planets and their
subordination to Christ's redemptive mission in the economy of
all creation will also bear on this question, and since the realization of such a possibility can not be even remotely verified at this
time there is no reason to clamor for an irrevocable decision. With
regard to contraception, I shall have more to say, when discussing
the apostasy of Charles Davis, on the disadvantages of pressing
for an "official" decision on this question.

What, then, do we expect as a result of the Council? I would
suggest that we anticipate a continuing impulse to be given by
the bishops to the entire spiritual awakening which the Christian
community has experienced in the last half century. This is a new
theological era, as has been said over and over in recent years:
this does not mean there is a "new theology" in the pejorative
sense. All theology is new: the Sacrament makes present; and
now is the acceptable time. And in point of fact the "new theological age" is no longer new chronologically. For we are moving
into the second stage of the modern Church, in which the achievements of the post-Vatican I — and more definitely, the achievements of the post-Modernist — period will be coordinated, sheared
of their extravagances, and given a new propulsion, new energy:
a stage in which flexibility will be a sign of mastery, and in which
the goal shall remain, as Blondel wrote to von Hügel, "not to
metamorphose the traditional data but to deepen them."[6]

Even in their American setting, religious doctrine and practice
are moving toward a moment of synthesis. The liturgical revival,
which in the hands of some of its more extreme partisans has
occasionally appeared excessively taken up with group or mass
participation, is now emphasizing the need for that communion
which has been defined as "alone with the Alone," and which

---

[6] Marle Op. cit., p. 148.

was rightly stressed in the Maritains' little book on prayer and contemplation.[7] Theology for the laity is becoming a genuinely theological discipline, truly illuminated by the revolutionary advances being made in scripture studies. Under the influence of kerygmatic catechetics the whole field of religious education from the primary grades up is being renovated. The "lay apostolate" is acquiring a fluidity of approach radically different from the rigid framework of its early days when European cadres of action were imported injudiciously, when such rudimentary notions as "think-judge-act" were subjected to a kind of rabbinic exegesis, and when the place of the Sodality in "Catholic Action" was a topic of urgent debate among American "militants." One awaits, then, a summation and a clarification of the efforts of the last half century.

In that deepening and freshening of our comprehension of traditional beliefs, which is the goal of the post-conciliar era, the insights of the present moment of history will be invaluable. For the whole drift of modern thought is away from the mechanistic orientation of the last three hundred years; and this personalist tenor has been reinforced by contemporary theological developments. The Church is less and less envisioned primarily as an institutional entity, nor is the bishop regarded as some kind of ecclesiastical manager. Even that sacrament which lends itself most readily to being defined in juridic terms, Penance, has been shown by Adrienne von Speyr to entail a personal encounter with the life of the Trinity.[8] The insights of personalism, of the meeting of the "self with the other," of the "I and thou," have been confirmed both in the doctrine of the Mystical Body and in the notion of Christ as the archetype of the sacraments. Indeed, so all-pervading are these insights that they are becoming the new slogans of the unthinking, and are engendering the kind of hot-house existentialism embalmed in the writings of Adrian van Kaam and Josef Goldbrunner.

It is, of course, difficult to detail how these various forces for renewal will affect the theology of the episcopal state, but there will obviously be consequences in the practical order deriving from a new sense of collegiality which ought to be examined.

---

[7] *Liturgy and Contemplation* (New York, 1960).

[8] *Confession: The Encounter with Christ in Penance* (New York, 1964).

First, one would expect over the next few decades the cardinalate to be reduced to a purely curial or honorary status (as presently with papal chamberlains), and the election of the Chief Bishop to be confined exclusively to certain bishops representing the episcopate of the whole Church. That an accident of medieval polity affecting the ancient See of Rome could in the twentieth century result in the election of the supreme teacher by members of the Church-taught is to depreciate both symbolically and in fact the episcopal college. How such a reform would be implemented is a minor consideration: possibly primatial sees, or — where none exists, as in this country — major dioceses would have attached to them the right of voting in conclave.

Second, the legal fiction of "titular" bishops could be discontinued. Auxiliary bishops now function mainly as subordinate governing officials or as ministers of Confirmation; but since the episcopal state is not primarily an administrative office, and since Confirmation need not be conferred by a bishop, this notion of a "titular" bishop reduces episcopal consecration to a kind of honorific. One remedy would be to allow lesser prelates to act as the bishops' auxiliaries, or — the preferable solution — to break up the larger dioceses so that titular bishops, unless coadjutors, could govern their own sees; the present meaningless situation in which a bishop may be pastor of a local parish could thus be terminated.

Both sociologically and liturgically a small diocese, composed of about fifteen or twenty parishes each with two hundred families, would be the ideal. This would allow for clearer and more direct lines of communication between the bishop and his priests, and for personal contact between layman and bishop. One inevitable and desirable consequence of this would be the democratizing of the episcopate. In place of the figure of a medieval princeling which the bishop now necessarily presents, inevitably engendering both in the bishop himself and in his people an authoritarian relationship, there would be the figure of a true shepherd of the flock; a figure akin to that of St. Paul who not only ruled and commanded but persuaded and cajoled, and who was occasionally himself the patient object of sharp remonstrance and frank criticism. Such a bishop of a small diocese could concelebrate on major feasts in a genuinely family gathering, and literally preach the word ex *cathedra* to all his people.

Although Karl Rahner has argued against the small diocese on the grounds that it cannot truly be a microcosm of the Church universal,[9] it may be suggested in rebuttal that his purely abstract theological line of reasoning must be subordinated to the preeminently pastoral demands of the present moment in the Church's history. Moreover, size provides no criterion for measuring the ecclesiologically representative character of a given diocese. Certainly the small primitive communities of Corinth and Jerusalem reflected all the variety of offices and functions that the Church as a whole displayed. Of course, in order to prevent the kind of numerical imbalance now exhibited by the Italian episcopate, such a dissolution of the large dioceses would have to take place in all Catholic countries within the same general period of time.

In the present situation where one bishop may rule over a million subjects there is very little opportunity for the rare and isolated prophetic voice to be heard. As a result public opinion can only with difficulty be mobilized — except through such eruptive methods as those used by Father Kavanaugh — and the latent *consensus fidelium* cannot be effectively articulated. Similarly — and now more relevant to such cases as those of Fathers DuBay and Coffield — if there were many small dioceses in one specific geographical area, a priest who found himself opposed to the policy of his own diocese would not have to make a complete break with his friends and associates, relocate to a distant place and uproot his entire ministerial career when transferring to another diocese. Lastly, the existence of many small dioceses would make inevitable the consecration of Negro priests, and thus put an end to the present scandalous situation in which — by contrast to many Protestant groups — no Negro is ordinary of an American diocese. Over a period of time a beneficial consequence of this would be that Negro bishops would be governing predominantly white dioceses.

This genuine democratizing of the episcopate is almost essential to the progress of the Church in the world of the twentieth century. Though the Church must remain, at least *de jure* a limited "monarchy," one may expect, as the collegiality of the bishops, and indeed the collegiality of the whole Church, is given

---

[9] "The Episcopate and the Primacy," *Inquiries* (New York, 1966), pp. 388 ff.

further impetus by the Council and the synod, that more and more the polymorphic structure of Catholicism will be intensified. As a result, a number of vexing questions will over the years be obviated.

For example, there has been much discussion in the journals on the need for a clearer proclamation on the relation of the Church to civil society than was offered by Vatican II. Some of those who have opposed such a proclamation may be merely defending the *status quo*, but the majority of this opposition bases its argument on the fact that a universally applicable declaration now would be premature and ineffectual. These latter believe that the relations between the Church and State throughout the world are so linked to different types of political regime and so intertwined with national traditions that any statement for the universal Church would have to be excessively qualified and vaguely worded, and thus in the end it would be diluted of any real significance.

This is a tenable position, since it is based on existing conditions throughout the Church and since it recognizes the dangers in succumbing to what one American theologian at Vatican I referred to as a "mania" for doctrinal declarations on every conceivable question.[10] The words of Kierkegaard are more than applicable here. "O Luther, thou hadst ninety-five theses; how terrible! But in a deeper sense, the more theses the less terrible."[11]

If the episcopate in each of the countries of the world reasserts its leadership, then the assembled bishops in each nation could speak with precision and clarity on the relationship of the Church to their own society. And so, too, with a number of other topics that have been advocated for the implementation of the Council's decrees. Many aspects of such issues as liturgical reform, parochial administration, a married priesthood, etc., can profitably be left to the decision of national hierarchies rather than be consigned to the judgment of Rome.

Besides the clarification of the doctrine of the episcopal office there is another reason for seeking an elaboration of the polymorphic principle in the Church. It is, basically, that by the interplay

---

[10] John Cardinal Farley, *Life of John Cardinal McCloskey* (New York, 1918), p. 276.

[11] *Attack upon Christendom* (Princeton, 1946), p. 32.

of varying and opposing orthodox views a fuller understanding
of revealed truth can result. What Newman called "freedom of
opinion" in the Church, and what Karl Rahner has called "free
speech" are expressions of the conviction that it is mainly by
the collision of contrary attitudes and ideals that new insights
emerge in the minds of individuals and groups. If this conviction
is justifiable then the goal of "dependent autonomy" must be
sought not only for the diocese in relation to the whole Church,
but also for certain groups and agencies within the individual
dioceses.

Two such agencies which could be allowed much more autonomy than they now exercise are the Catholic universities and
the major monastic foundations. In the case of the latter, the
right of the abbey *nullius* or of the religious house directly subject to the Holy See could be extended to many well-established
communities. And this would be in line with the historical evolution of American monasticism. In the nineteenth century when
St. Vincent's in Pennsylvania and New Melleray in Iowa sought
to have their priors made abbots, almost every bishop who was
consulted opposed the change in status. Yet in spite of that opposition there are today in this country scores of mitred abbots
whose communities cooperate fully with the local bishop in the
common apostolate. It is now perhaps time to carry this development of interdependence one stage further.

Similarly, one would like to see a greater autonomy for our
major universities. "There was true private judgment in the primitive and medieval schools — there are no schools now,"[12] wrote
Newman a hundred years ago. The great medieval universities,
Paris, Oxford, Bologna were, in their relation and friction with
other sectors of the Church, forces for progress both in ideas and
in action. The modern counterparts of those great Catholic
universities, by sharing in this same polymorphic principle, could
fulfill a comparable role today. But that Notre Dame must accommodate the whims of the Bishop of Fort Wayne, Loyola,
those of Cardinal Cody, and Fordham, those of Archbishop Cooke
— that this should be the situation facing every independent
Catholic college or university is a direct contradiction of the
principle of collegiality.

[12] Ward, *op. cit.*, I, p. 588.

This principle, which theologically underlies the polymorphic conception of the Church, has been subject to some criticism as a consequence of the widespread discussion of Rolf Hochhuth's *Der Stellvertreter*.[13] And it has been suggested that the major reason for the silence of Pius XII on Hitler's genocidal policy was his sympathetic responsiveness to the sentiments of the German hierarchy. Thus John Lukacs has written:

Had there been more responsibility vested in the German national hierarchy, had the Mass been offered in German for a generation, wouldn't the record of German Catholicism during the war have been even more pitiful? Was the problem of the German Catholics that they were hopelessly outdated, out of line with the modern national development of Germany? Was it not, rather, that their rhetoric and their political beliefs fitted in very well with that development? Who was a sturdier opponent of Hitler, the old traditionalist Pius XI or his in many respects more modern and up-to-date successor? Wasn't the problem precisely that the authority of the Holy Father was not sufficiently paternal, not sufficiently authoritative, not sufficiently universal? Isn't it true that what the world needed then, and what many of us (including Hochhuth) expect now is something quite different from an august spiritual chairman of the board of an international organization of national companies, that the world is looking for someone whose singular authority should have spoken to us in a strong and clear voice: the Representative, the Vicar of Christ, the Sovereign standing on the rock of Peter?[14]

The only answer that can be proffered to this impassioned series of questions is the traditional one which affirms that ideally a monarchy may be the best form of government from the viewpoint of execution of laws, but that from the viewpoint of the formulation of laws a democracy is preferable. One could accept Professor Lukacs' conclusions only if one were so to exaggerate the supernatural guidance of the Holy See as to view it as incapable of political error. Since the whole of history contradicts this notion, one is compelled to repeat the truism that there is more wisdom in the collective judgment of many prudent men over the long run than in the individual judgment of only one. If the Papacy were some utterly trans-temporal and ahistorical institution, if the Pope were some utterly detached and objective observer, completely without any racial or national prejudices, then one might prefer his judgment to that of all the episcopates in the Church universal. But in fact the Pope in Rome is as much the subject of political pressures, is as necessarily caught up in the experiences of a given geographical situation, is as liable to succumb to purely religious biases as any national hierarchy. Given this parallel submission to historical conditions on the part of an episcopal synod and of the papacy the only ground for preferring the judgment of the former to that of the latter in temporal affairs is the wider range of sentiment and information available to it.

Turning now from these practical considerations on the reform of the episcopal office, it is necessary to look at the fundamental theological doctrine that must inspire any such reform. According to one of the best commentaries in English on ecclesiastical law (Abbo and Hannan) the common opinion of canonists is that the bishop should be more skilled in canon law than learned in theology. This judgment may indicate special pleading on the part of canonists, but one suspects rather that its general acceptance is an effect of that denigration of the episcopate which Cardinal Manning decried. The bishop becomes in that misconception not a teacher in his own right, but merely the emissary of the Pope. And through this distortion of traditional teaching, he becomes in this country the victim of those arrogant attacks on the "Roman hierarchy" as the "Vatican foreign service," which still emanate from Protestants and Others and from the half-lights of the Beacon Press. But these attacks may be as much the result of the failure of theologians to explicate Catholic teaching as of prejudice on the part of non-Catholics. For Catholic teaching affirms that the bishop is not the Pope's vicar, much less his ambassador; he is the one teacher of his *ecclesia*, and as a member of the episcopal college he is a teacher of the universal Church in union with its Chief Bishop.

Might not one further suggest that it has been this notion of the bishop as an interpreter of the law rather than as a teacher of doctrine which accounts for the not infrequent silence of some bishops on pressing social and ethical issues? If the bishop is the chief teacher of Christian truth, he is also its chief witness; but if he is regarded as an interpreter of the law, his proper domain is jurisprudence, not testimony to truth. It is not desirable to discount any claims of prudence; but to make them the over-riding consideration, and to define the episcopal office in terms of them, may tend to induce a muteness that occasionally verges on the scandalous — as I believe it has in the Council's declaration on antisemitism. The "church of silence" is not always behind the iron curtain; it existed quite obviously in Hitler's Germany and even in parts of this country today. Furthermore, a witness is a martyr. This martyrdom may not be a murder in the cathedral; it may take the more harrowing form of public criticism as in the case of Bishop Reed of Oklahoma City; it may take the form of the antagonism of some of the bishop's brethren; it may take the form — as it did in more than a few instances at the time of Vatican I — of rebuke by the Pope; or it may take the form of loss of one's see, as in the case of Archbishop Charbonneau in this hemisphere. But may not this be the price of accepting the plenitude of the priesthood, and of being the successor of the apostles?

Surely it is past the time to say that for the bishops merely to reiterate the just-war doctrine without making any effort to determine if it is actually being applied in Vietnam, is to make an utterance touching on the bathetic. Who shouts nothing from the housetops? The issue of civilian bombing or torture of prisoners is a moral one, and it ought to be apparent that the official front-line defenders of Christian morality should not be so overwhelmed by what they view as the exigencies of prudence as to fail to take the lead in resolving it. In order to avoid alienating Catholics whose adhesion to Catholic teaching is merely nominal — and whose alienation is their own freely chosen responsibility — a situation has arisen in which the very fulfillment of this Catholic teaching is frustrated.

However, it must be said in all fairness that the American Church has been graced with bishops who for the most part were sympathetic to the legitimate aspirations of the community, and who, particularly from the time of Gibbons and Ireland, have identified themselves with the cause of social justice. Unfortunately in recent decades these were often causes initiated outside the Church, and the hierarchy merely gave its approbation to movements already sanctioned by public opinion. But at least our bishops have not been mere ceremonial functionaries; there have been eminent theologians and humanists among them, such as the two Kenricks and Spalding of Peoria. And coming from the ranks of the middle-class, they have very rarely been intent on that social display enshrined in Archbishop Seton's monument to ecclesiastical snobbism, *Memories of Many Years*; nor have they been afflicted with that passion for personal aggrandizement which led Léon Bloy to observe of an eminent prelate: "The Cardinal had a heart of gold. Solid gold."

But one regrets having to state that the bishops have not always exercised that leadership which their personal qualities, their educational training, and their consecration authorized. This failure has stemmed both from that lack of "self-knowledge" which the truncated theology of 1870 induced, and from the same difficulties of articulation and communication that beset the heads of all large institutions and corporations: they are faced with the problem of keeping in vital contact with all the echelons of their organization. And it is here that the layman can play an important role. If the present immense dioceses are not going to be broken up, then some formalized instrument must be established so that the bishop, who now necessarily moves in a circle of high public officials and of people of wealth and power, may hear the word of the layman, and may encounter through him the issues before the mass of the Christian community. I say "formalized instrument" because the present make-shift arrangement of communion breakfasts or Holy Name affairs or semi-solemn receptions, or even the presence of the layman on the staffs of some diocesan papers, is much too indirect and haphazard to result in any real communication. There is a parallel to the kind of formal institution of the dialogue being suggested here in the quinquennial assemblies at which the bishops gathered with the lower clergy in the Church of France before the revolution — the gap between bishop and clergy at that period being greater than the gap between hierarchy and laity in the present age. Or similarly one may find a parallel in the kind of "oblique" place the layman held at earlier ecumenical councils through the presence at them of representatives from the great Catholic universities. One would like, for instance, to see the various recently founded "associations of laymen" represented at the meetings of the USBC or at diocesan synods: and this, not merely as the spokesman of the narrow conception of the "lay apostolate," but as the voice of all the interests and hopes of the Church, as seen from the vantage of the lay state.

This will certainly strip away some of the vestigial protocol and panoply that now encumber the bishop in the exercise of his office. And it means that the layman's testimony is not always going to be couched in diplomatic niceties. The layman must speak vigorously and clearly; indeed, this vigor and clarity are the outward signs of his inward commitment to the cause of the Church in the temporal order, and they ought not to be interpreted as indications of a lack of obedience or docility. One of the great moral theologians of the twentieth century, Werner Schoellgen, has explained the indifference of some German bishops to the monstrousness of Hitler's regime by the laity's failure to inform them of it. "The laity looked to spiritual 'leaders' on whom they could lay all the burden of responsibility."[15] There may be some truth in this, but I imagine the failure was reciprocal. The layman is rarely going to continue to proffer his testimony if it is ignored or if the only apparent response it elicits is a reprimand for effrontery and lack of "respect."

The bishop is a pontiff: a builder of bridges. One of the bridges that must be repaired is that between hierarchy and laity. This is not now a matter of democracy, or of prudent government; it is a theological and ecclesiological imperative. If the layman is not heard, the bishops can have no awareness of the true consensus of the faithful; moreover if the layman in this age of democracy is ignored by the hierarchy, he will gradually ignore it in turn. He will confine his relationship to the Church to a minimal one of receiving the sacraments and contributing to the local parish. His intellect and interests which can find channels in abundance in the secular world will simply atrophy so far as his religious concerns go.

Kerk en ruimte is a pregnant Dutch phrase which means an "open" Church, or better, a "roomy" Church; a Church which, as Newman said, allows "elbow room for the mind," for controversy, for honest differences, and for the gesture of obedience, and the Sign of the Cross.

---

[15] Werner Schoellgen, Moral Problems Today (New York, 1963), p. 141.

III

PRIESTS IN THE WORLD

Well over a century ago, Abbé de Lamennais, traveling back from Rome where his democratic views had been condemned by the highest ecclesiastical authorities, stopped in Munich to meet with a relatively unknown priest-historian, Ignaz von Döllinger. De Lamennais then continued on to Paris and shortly afterwards wrote *Paroles d'un croyant*, a book in which he described a satanic conclave assembled to uproot "religion, science, and thought," and to destroy "Christ Who has restored liberty to the world." The allegory seemed transparently antipapal and anticurial, and the book was condemned by Gregory XVI as being "tiny in size but immense in perversity," and its author, who had been characterized by one of Gregory's predecessors as "the last of the Fathers," was gradually "hounded out of the Church" — to use Wilfrid Ward's phrase.[1]

Around this time a young Anglican cleric in a bitter polemic entitled "The Fall of M. de La Mennais," attacked the Abbé for seeming to "believe in the existence of certain indefeasible rights of man." Nearly half a century later this same cleric, who only gradually came to realize that de Lamennais had been doing "a service to religion,"[2] also planned on stopping in Munich on his way back from Rome where he had been raised to the cardinalate by Leo XIII, and he too intended to meet with Dr. Döllinger. Cardinal Newman hoped to persuade Döllinger to accept the

---

[1] Cf. Charles Sylvain, *Grégoire XVI* (Paris, 1899), p. 193; *Life and Letters of John Lingard*, ed. Martin Haile and Edward Bonney (St. Louis, 1913), p. 226; Maisie Ward, *The Wilfrid Wards and the Transition* (New York, 1934), p. 317.

[2] John Henry Cardinal Newman, *Essays Critical and Historical* (London, 1891), p. 157; Ward, *Life*, I, p. 484.

Vatican decrees. But Newman's intention, as we know, was never fulfilled, and Döllinger, like de Lamennais before him, died an outcast from the Church which he had so long served.

Both Döllinger and de Lamennais were men born out of due time. For if a doctrine of collegiality, such as that which Vatican II affirmed, had been proclaimed in 1870, there would have been no Old Catholic schism and no defection by Dr. Döllinger; if the principles of freedom of conscience proclaimed at the fourth session of the last Council had been tolerated by churchmen in the early nineteenth century, there would have been no tragedy of de Lamennais.

There are many morals to be drawn from this narrative, not the least of which is that the second Vatican Council should not be praised too extravagantly for having embraced the age of reason, for endorsing views — e.g., the decree on religious liberty — which have largely been commonplaces among secular humanists for a hundred and fifty years. But the more immediate lesson of this historical parable has to do with the manner in which de Lamennais, Döllinger, and Newman responded to the encroachments of an abusive ecclesiastical authority.

No theme runs more constantly through Newman's Catholic years than that of the need for bringing sure truths into line with historical conditions — one of those conditions being in Newman's own time an indisposition on the part of Pio Nono to accept even the surest of truths. Faced by the condemnation of some of his most deeply held convictions, Newman could have, like de Lamennais and Döllinger, continued to press his claims. That he didn't was not a matter of expediency, was not a mere tactical maneuver, but was the result of a conviction that once he had borne his witness as vigorously as possible it was not for him to attempt to force circumstances, to attempt to bend the times to his own will.

With the exception of Scheeben and Dupanloup, no nineteenth-century Catholic thinker had so profound an understanding of the layman's role as had Newman. And Newman believed that the work of applying the principles enunciated by ordained teachers — whether official voices such as the bishops or prophetic voices such as Newman himself — devolved primarily upon the laity.

Thus there can be recognized a threefold martyrdom for priest, bishop, and pope when they witness to truth: it involves not only the actual giving of testimony, but also the obloquy to which they may as a result be subject and the personal frustration they may experience at not being able *actively to implement* the truths which they have discerned. Here lies the only possible solution to the dilemma in which Hochhuth saw Pius XII trapped. When acting in that shadowy realm where prudential judgments are made, the consecrated minister of Christ cannot afford to temporize, cannot seek to accommodate his testimony to the demands of the practical order: precisely as an heir of the apostles his absolutely first duty, transcending that of administration and government, is to bear witness no matter what consequences may follow. The consecrated minister simply must not be solicitous for the morrow when it is a question of fidelity to his primary role as herald and witness, of fidelity to his kerygmatic and martyrial office.

What, though, if his confession is ignored — which is an entirely different thing from its not being heard? For if it is a *genuine* confession it will be heard, and whether or not it is ignored, the witness will have fulfilled his obligation as successor of the apostles. For what he proclaims is the seed-bearing word, and if the seed falls on bad ground, this is not his primary concern, because no matter where the seed falls, no matter who sows it, it is not he who gives the increase, but God who brings it to fruition through other secondary causes. This is the glory and the tragedy of the ordained witness: it is the burden of his cross that having been raised so high as priest, he must experience his creatureliness, even more deeply perhaps than does the layman, by not being directly able to translate his word into action. Whereas the layman who hears the word has an obligation to seek to bring the times into joint with it, to act and manipulate, to maneuver and agitate to the end that whatever refractory matter may be standing as an obstacle to the word shall be brought into conformity with it.

Here, then, is the theological basis for Archbishop Rummel's reply to a group of laymen who had asked him to implement his earlier statements on integration: "It's your move, gentlemen; you know the state of mind of the people as well as I do. You create the atmosphere necessary for the success of such a move and I'll make it."[3] And if it is said, in the case of integrating schools owned by a diocese, that it is only the bishop who can effectively act in this area, then one must counter by asserting that this provides merely another of many good reasons for bishops and priests to get out of the business of administering schools.

This is to say quite simply that the ordained are committed primarily to the proclamation of the one truth, and that the laity has as mission to elevate the multiplicity of matter that it may touch this unity of spirit which is, as it were, reaching down from on high. The ordained, then, after having borne their emphatic witness to spirit must put their faith in that spirit, and in its ultimately non-frustrable character; they must have faith in the movement of Christ through time and with a sense of detached commitment believe that the errors of today will inevitably be corrected tomorrow. They therefore must follow in the steps of Newman and not of de Lamennais.

It is the layman who should apply the confession of the bishop and his delegates to the concrete order. The layman *as a rule* has not the charism of clear theological discernment: that pertains to the bishop's office. And in this is the tragedy and glory of the layman's cross. He does not clearly see; he can, so to speak, only hear and act. But by his very vocation to the world of *action*, the layman must be literally im-*patient*, must refuse to place his trust in some distant future. By his very mission to the temporal, the layman cannot ordinarily place himself above time and disinterestedly expect that the seed-bearing word will grow without his culture of its soil.

These truisms have an obvious relevance to recent events in this country. There have been priests and even bishops who have heroically borne their witness to truth and who have had as a consequence indignities heaped upon them by the ecclesiastical machinery. But that is only a slight part of their cross: the greater straitening is that they must, having fully preached their word, leave it to others to actualize it in the practical order. The witness of the word differs from the witness of the deed — ordinarily (for obviously, there is a prophetic spirit in the Church which dissolves these distinctions). But in the general case — and that

---

[3] William Osborne, *The Segregated Covenant* (New York, 1966), p. 124.

is the only kind that admits of being discussed — the priest who
seeks to force circumstances to conform to his confession of faith
violates his own vocation, laicizes himself in his heart, and ultimately, because of this corruption of values, becomes thoroughly
committed to the temporal sphere.

Of course, the priest must also be a doer of the word, but this
doing must be in those areas where the physical has already been
brought into a condition of malleability by the layman, where
the fully concrete and pragmatic has been opened up by the
layman to that influx of spirit which the priest's subsequent
actions shall then increase. Reciprocally the layman by his very act
of attending to the word will begin to shape the matter of his
daily affairs, and this matter he is shaping — in response to the
testimony of the ordained — will, as it moves from its state of
crude mass, elicit from the official teachers that clearer and more
precise witnessing which the layman can only provide inchoately,
and which can only be manifest faintly through the density of
the physical world which is his proper ambiance.

The priest who lets these orders be inverted almost invariably
falls victim to the kind of otherwise admirable humanism proclaimed by a Loisy or a Friedrich Heiler; similarly the layman
inverting his vocation may find himself propounding the kind of
ritualized humanitarianism elaborated by an Auguste Comte. Both
natural religions syncretize — that of the fallen priest and that of
the self-ordained layman — for when radical distinctions of office
are destroyed a common greyness smothers everything.

Let the layman attend to the truth-bearing witness of the priest
— even if in *extraordinary* cases such witness contradicts that of
his bishop, since it is the truth that counts; let the priest who has
borne his witness, when the matter at hand does not admit of
being readily shaped by his word, silently inspire (by definition,
there is no other kind of inspiration) the layman's active penetration of the world of the intractable. This is implicit in all our
notions of hierarchy, of participationism, and of subsidiarity.

It is perhaps at this point that the dialectic tension between
the eschatological and the incarnational dimension of Christianity
can be best defined. The primary mission of the Church is not
that of "saving souls" or "making converts," much less that of
alleviating human misery or civilizing mankind; rather, it is simply

to be the sign before the world of the second coming of Christ. However important all other actions of the Church and of church-men may be, these actions are only secondary in relation to this signifying forth before all peoples of Christ's return in glory. But if the Church is to be truly this effective sign, she must in turn make use of the "signs of the time," she must make use of those dispositions and aptitudes in the here and now concrete reality — in mundo huius temporis, as the conciliar decree has it — which make it receptive to the witnessing Word. And in the discern-ment of these signs of this time, the layman plays the major role. By his very state he is best able to interpret the events of the present moment as well as to transform the temporal so that it is conformable to the Word which "comes down from on high."

Not only because of all the reasons given above must the lay-man shoulder the greater responsibility in the active struggle for the transfiguration of matter by spirit, but also because it is an empiric datum that the layman cannot be as deeply wounded by the highest authorities as can the priest who is in every way closer to those authorities. Is it not an equally empiric fact that the priest who has been laicized whether in reality or in his heart (and making many exceptions for that prophetic call which only the individual himself can judge), who has let his sacerdotal character be blurred, only obliquely serves the cause to which he has been dedicated? It is a clear lesson of history that the priest cut off from the spouse — the Church through his bishop — to whom he has been wed by ordination becomes involute, turned in upon himself because he has lost his true "other," and that as a consequence his person itself becomes gradually deformed as his vision grows more and more distorted. The contrast between Acton and Döllinger, von Hügel and Loisy, between Montalem-bert and de Lamennais would point up the validity of this general conclusion.

At this point one might well wonder whether it is permissible to write in this way, seemingly to scrutinize the agonies of good men and dispassionately to adjudicate the most fundamental con-flict faced by the human person. To that the answer can only be a qualified and hesitant "yes," and this because we do not know whether the struggles of public or historical figures are more significant than are the private ones we all must face, and because we *do* know that exceptions — even in a religion founded on exceptions — remain just that: exceptions; and if some or any guidelines can be drawn, it is all to the good.

One may also wonder where does this leave such active priestly works as the *Mission de France*, the "équipe de Gerland," and the projects of the *Economie et Humanisme* team. The answer can only be that it leaves them much where they are: in their state as bearers of a living witness. But it is on the *witnessing* that the stress must be placed. There is not much doubt that the ill-fated condemnation of the priest workers could have been based on the sound theoretical assumption that the priests had identified themselves too closely with the proletariat as proletariat; that is, that they had adopted for the most apostolic of motives the Marxist doctrine on the relation of the proletariat to the exploiting class. Such adoption no doubt led to their closer identification with the cause of the workers; but it also implied that the priests would have to play a part in any and all, well-founded or ill-founded, campaigns against the *patronat*.

Since in Marx the very notion of proletariat v. bourgeoisie *necessarily* implies an active struggle, it is evident that the worker-priests' identification with the "proletariat" as a sociological category entailed considerably more than their mere identification with the workers as such. One may suspect that it was not this theoretical realization that the sacerdotal office was being obscured which led to the condemnation of the *Mission de France*, but only the fact that the employers, fearing the presence of well-trained men committed to the cause of the workers, brought pressure to bear on the Curia. Nevertheless the theoretical distinction is basic. The role of the priest worker is not immediately that of active implementation of the principles of justice, but rather that of bearing witness to such justice. The form of witness is in itself irrelevant whether by one's work or by one's speech or by both; what is relevant and supremely so, is that any work done is done simply that it may be an effective instrument for the witnessing, and not primarily that it may achieve some tangible result in the world of temporal affairs. The danger for the priest in this country with regard to civil rights as in France with regard to the workers has been that the temporal goals may assume priority.

It is for this reason that Bishop Alfred Ancel, who even as a bishop had been a factory worker, prescribed for the members of his group the rule that: "In order to assure himself of maintaining a truly priestly comportment in the worker's milieu, the priest *should abstain from all temporal commitment whatever it may be* and he should enter into the activities of his fellow workers only with a view to those priestly functions which constitute his proper ministry"[4] (original italics). The meaning of this — and it has a direct relation to recent efforts of priests to bear their own courageous witness whether with regard to Vietnam or the civil-rights crisis — is brought out in the following from Msgr. Ancel: "Strictly speaking, a priest has no more right to make himself a worker than to make himself a bourgeois, though certain apostolic needs may lead him to work in a factory, even as other apostolic needs might lead priests to study middle-class culture in order to be better able to know the men who have been formed by that culture."[5]

The great danger in the priest's making a total commitment to the goods of the temporal order is that he begins to work toward the realization of these temporal goods primarily. He loses what Bishop Ancel calls the "universalism of the priesthood" and what Yves Congar in *Vraie et fausse réforme* called "communion with the whole."[6] Both "universalism" and "communion" imply spirit: and precisely what happens to the priest as a result of his loss is that he begins to invade the layman's domain which is that of pragma and multiplicity. As we move lower down on the hierarchic scale of any institutional structure — there is no such thing as an institution *without* hierarchy — works become diversified: that is, the lay role is specialized. (It is one of the more grievous enormities of certain militant lay-edited publications that they have focused the attention even of the well-intentioned exclusively on insular problems, however tragic these may be: that these journals have appeared intent on goading clerics on into that world of action where the layman should by right bear the brunt of the struggle and confront the abuses of an arrogant authority.)

As the priest loses more and more his hold on universal values,

---

[4] *Cinq ans avec les ouvriers* (Lyons, 1964), p. 124.

[5] *Ibid.*, p. 317.

[6] Paris, 1950, pp. 264 ff.

the local situations, no matter how evil in themselves, and concrete problems peculiar to a given area, loom more and more in
his mind as the central realities. He is then tempted to cut himself off from the bishop — ordinarily indefensible no matter how
recalcitrant and personally obnoxious such a bishop may have
proved himself to be — and ultimately he may find himself in fact
as well as in heart in the lay state. Having lost this "communion
with the whole" he may then begin to let himself be tempted
against the Church itself.

Msgr. Ancel has anatomized this temptation in *5 ans avec les
ouvriers*; and though he is writing with a view to French conditions, only few substitutions of language are needed to apply
what he has said to scores of situations in this country:

Living in the midst of non-Christians who are sociologically cut off
from the Church, who regard it as a stranger and usually as an adver-
sary, who criticize it continually in its leaders and in its members, one
suffers almost fatally the temptation of breaking off (*désolidariser*)
completely from what one is criticizing.

I would like to attempt to describe this temptation and show how
it invades little by little the spirit and the whole being of those who
are not able to surmount it.

In the beginning one does not wish to break with the Church, but
only with what is evil in it; but if one is not on his guard one lets
oneself be drawn progressively by the sociological current in which
one is immersed, and little by little the word "Church" evokes the
same reactions that it evokes in the world of the worker. By that very
fact one is tempted to revolt against the evil which exists in the
Church.

One seeks to justify this revolt by thinking that this evil frustrates
those who are working for Christ. Then, one no longer understands
why the Pope and the bishops happen to tolerate all this evil. One
does not understand how the parish clergy are able to render themselves more or less complicit in this evil. Little by little one grows
hardened; one criticizes, one attacks, and finally one feels oneself
more at home among one's fellow workers in their sociological anti-
clericalism than with the clergy and practicing Catholics in their
attachment to the Church; for, one rationalizes, so long as the Church
remains what it is, one is able to do nothing as a missionary.

The result of this temptation is that one is led to pursue a path
independent of the Church with a view to leading to Christ one's
fellow workers of good will . . . despite the Church.[7]

Is not this the present peril? Is not the priest in danger of

---

[7] *Op. cit.*, p. 309.

identifying his successes in various social movements with successes in his ministry of witnessing, and of sacrificing the latter to the former?

And have we not seen the outcome of this temptation in too many cases? In Father Feeney's obsession with a dead ecclesiological maxim and an exaggerated Marian doctrine; in Emmett McLoughlin's noble but narrow preoccupation with the administration of charitable works; in Boyd Barrett's concern with the collision of a new science and an old theology; and in the Tyrrells, and in the Davises and the Loisys, and in so many more heroic but constricted visionaries — of whom few have have been able, like Boyd Barrett, to recapture later that vision of the whole which defines Catholicism. One can only hope, then, that the example of a Father George Dunne, and more recently of a Father John Coffield, will be operative in the scandalous atmosphere that Cardinal McIntyre coninues to let prevail in his see city.

I would close with some words of Yves Congar written at the time of the excommunication of a small group of French Catholics, led by Abbé Jean Massin and calling themselves "The Community of Christian Hope." These words are all the more significant because Congar himself was pilloried by clerical delators and censors for having been in part responsible, through *Vraie et fausse réforme*, for Abbé Massin's defection. And these words take on an even greater weight because Congar has recently sketched in *Chrétiens en dialogue* the mistrust and even contempt shown during the fifties by Roman authorities towards himself and some of the most dedicated and saintly figures of the postwar French religious revival.[8] That he and his confreres, though bending, never broke under the lash of Rome makes his testimony utterly probative. Congar wrote:

One is able to leave the Church. But after that, what then? I have here before me a number of manifestoes: that of the liberal Catholic Church, of the Kingdom of God, of the Evangelical Catholic Church, of the French Evangelical Church, and of many others. Several of these groups which in their time have caused much suffering and trouble to souls no longer exist. What have they achieved in the final analysis but to break with the Faith and to render more difficult the work of the Gospel in the world? Does not history cry out with

---

[8] Paris, 1964.

all its might at the vanity of trying to purify the Church against itself? In forty or fifty years, when others shall overtake us on the paths of our present cares, those who today destroy and rebuild in the flower of their twenty or thirty years shall be not only ignored but forgotten. Where shall they be? What shall they believe? Reading the manifesto of their youth, I fear that they find nothing great in the profound truths which the saints have lived in the Church and for which at this very moment confessors are offering without glory before the eyes of men, their health, their liberty, and the very life of the body.[9]

Congar had faith in history and faith in the power of spirit ultimately to reform the distortions and errors which he saw about him. That he did not react violently to the suppression of *Vraie et fausse réforme* and many other writings has resulted in his achievement's bearing now in these more propitious times — which ten years ago were completely unforeseeable — the richest and most lasting fruit. The present Pope has stated publicly that the works of Congar had nurtured his own spirit and had instructed him in the ways of religious renewal. It is no small thing to be a teacher of popes.

---

[9] *Témoignage Chrétien* (January 11, 1952).

IV

CHARLES DAVIS:
THE GLAMOUR OF DISSENT

In December of 1966, a few journalists instinctively confecting the senecan pap their craft makes mandatory and reciting to themselves the tag, "English Cleric Abandons Church," concluded immediately: Davis=Newman. No one outside their trade took this aphoristic history to heart, and no one not of a like univocal temper (e.g., Garry Wills for whom all "conservatives" are opposed to all "liberals" on all points of life and thought, worship and dogma) could have imagined that somehow the reporters' tidy parallel illuminated the low state to which the entire body of the Catholic faithful had sunk.[1] It was obvious that no parallel on any substantial point could be drawn, and that none will be drawn along those lines until Charles Davis produces his own equivalent of the *Essay on Development* (and this has not been achieved in *A Question of Conscience*). That will be a task of some magnitude since Charles Davis' theology now seems to allow little play to the institutional embodiments of an ideology, to Newman's Leitmotiv of a primordial unity that shapes its implicities — a Leitmotiv that Loisy saw applicable to the entire religious evolution of humanity.[2]

---

[1] With lavish piety Garry Wills wrote: "One does no service to Davis by comparing him with Newman. One simply discredits one's own judgment. Indeed, the challenge to the Church is not presented by Father Davis' sad loss, but by the intellectual character of the response to it. The Church must survive defections, and it will. It will survive the even severer challenge of its own members' wearying silliness. Looking at Father Davis, I pray for him. Looking at those who answered him, I pray for us." "Astonishing Reactions to Davis," *The National Catholic Reporter* (January 25, 1967).

[2] *Mémoires pour servir à l'histoire religieuse de notre temps* (Paris, 1930), I, p. 426.

But one should not be too hard on the religion editors of our weeklies; even the witless evocation of the nineteenth century with regard to the Davis affair may open up a fruitful image to explore. For as one reads Father Davis' *Observer* exposé (and, later, his book-length statement of his reasons for leaving the Church), one has the impression confirmed that what he is rebelling against is largely a spectre out of the era of Pio Nono. In the Roman Catholic Church, Fr. Davis finds "no attention to truth for its own sake." The accusation is that of Canon Charles Kingsley in 1864: "Truth for its own sake had never been a virtue with the Roman clergy." It is most strange, however, that Fr. Davis should choose to buttress his assertion by a discussion of the postponement of a papal decision on contraception. "To say, as the Pope did, that the teaching authority of the Church was not in a state of doubt on the issue of birth control was to deny a plain fact."

Now, a great deal of tender solicitude towards Fr. Davis, as is only fitting, has been displayed in all Catholic commentaries on his defection (save for the spastic anachronisms of *Triumph*); and potentially critical onlookers rightly have been warned of the imperatives of charity, of how one must accept Fr. Davis at his word, must not pass judgment on his inner motives, etc. Such is the glamour of dissent. It is characteristic of the present state of the Church, for which there are good (nineteenth century) reasons, that in self-exoneration one may publicly read into papal conduct a "callous dishonesty," all the while expecting others to take one's own conduct at its immediate face value. This is but another form of that philo-laicism to which I refer elsewhere in this book in a discussion of Catholic universities;[3] only now the phenomenon expands to philo-plebeianism: the man in authority is always deceptive; the man in the ranks is always a model of candor — and one forgets that both are merely men seeking somehow to work their way out of a muddle as best their training, intelligence, circumstances will allow.

Fr. Davis' advancing the contraception issue as his personal crux is a little surprising since at no time had he indicated any overriding concern about this question which has been vexing the Catholic community for a decade now, and toward the reso-

[3] Cf. *Infra*, p. 115.

lution of which a number of clerics equally as subject to episcopal sanction as he have been heroically spending themselves. Even more surprising is the onus he attaches to the papal statement that there "existed no doubt" on the matter. How can anyone say this is false, since it is readily conceivable that while there may be no doubt whatever on the issue itself, there may be great doubt as to the advisability of rendering a decision immediately? It suggests a kind of radical gnosticism to ignore the pastoral consequences, the institutional turbulence that will result from a definitive decision on contraception, whether favorable or unfavorable. Certainly this is not the first time that religious affirmations have been acknowledged as correct, but opposed as untimely and imprudent — at Vatican I the entire liberal party almost unanimously based its public opposition to defining papal infallibility on its "inopportunism." As Newman said: "The Church moves as a whole; it is not a mere philosophy, it is a communion; it not only discovers, but it teaches; it is bound to consult for charity as well as for faith. You must prepare men's minds for the doctrine, and you must not flout and insult the existing traditions of countries."[4]

What Fr. Davis reads as a "bureaucratic insensitivity to people and their sufferings," seems superficially to merit sympathy — though one must add one would have liked to see that insensitivity being corrected by more of England's theologians a few years ago. But in fact it may be precisely a concern for "people and their suffering" which motivates the postponement that caused Fr. Davis his "climax of revulsion." Anyone not isolated from concrete pastoral affairs, anyone, that is, who has much to do either with parish priests or with their parishioners knows how much confusion, bewilderment, and even moral relativism might be presently induced by any decision on contraception.[5] And against the "people and their suffering" must be weighed the fact that through selective prejudices large numbers of Catholics are already suggesting that if the Church can change her position on contraception, she can change on other issues, on, for in-

---

[4] Wilfrid Ward, *Life*, II, p. 296.

[5] The example of Vatican I is illuminating: cf. Archbishop Peter Kenrick, "I feared in certain parts of Europe, especially, that such a definition might lead to the dangers of schism in the Church." John O'Shea, *The Two Kenricks* (Philadelphia, 1909), p. 333.

stance, racial segregation, antisemitism, and noncombatant immunity.[6] To this, it could of course be replied that a mature secular humanism should be enough to correct these inhuman aberrations. Regrettably, the evils of segregation, mass murder of civilians, and antisemitism demand correction now, and there is no time to wait for an undeveloped humanism to provide it. It is not enough blandly to assert concerning such possible consequences of a favorable decision on contraception: so what? leave the bewilderment, confusion, etc., to the Holy Spirit to solve. For the spirit acts only through institutions, through men with sensibilities, idiosyncrasies, biases; in short, acts only through men with histories.

There is much to be said for being aware of the wholeness of the Church, for taking into account the problems radical moral reforms may generate in seemingly unrelated areas: there is little to be said in favor of an ecclesiology founded on a villain-theory, even if the villain is masked under such epithets as "system" and "institution." Because the witness of such as Archbishop Roberts and Canon Drinkwater is clearly born of communion with the whole Church on all its levels, it is so much more effective than the fervid though tardy expressions of anguish Fr. Davis has voiced. There is an obvious danger that anyone in a highly specialized office will lose sight of the totality; for if the Church is anything it is neither curia nor hierarchy, but parish and the new forms of community that the parish will give rise to; it is above all not seminary life nor theological speculation where for reasons good and bad the heel of authority grinds most ruthlessly.

It is, of course, an arrogant cliché for the pious to say that intellectuals are out of touch with reality and victims of self-infatuation: one thinks immediately of Fernand Hayward on Dr. Döllinger: ". . . a university professor of great learning, but also of excessive pride."[7] Nevertheless, the stereotyped Roman Catholic

---

[6] With regard to noncombatant immunity, William V. O'Brien has observed of its alleged obsolescence: "Moreover, as we seem to be discovering in other problem areas such as population, it may be that the traditional way of formulating the issues and judging them are neither adequate nor obligatory" (italics added). "After Nineteen Years Let Us Begin," Worldview (December, 1964). For critique see Justus George Lawler, Nuclear War: The Ethics, the Rhetoric, the Reality (Westminster, 1965), p. 70.

[7] The Vatican Council (Dublin, 1951), p. 49.

apology that contrasts the proud de Lamennais with the humble Lacordaire, the proud Loisy with the humble Laberthonnière[8] is not entirely without foundation; and it was wise counsel that the great master of the spiritual life, Abbé Huvelin, gave to Baron von Hügel, that most cerebral of Catholics, that he should pray the rosary daily to help prevent his "interior life from losing touch with the devotion of the people."[9] But this is a delicate area, and the whole matter of personal piety v. pride relates so closely to what is utterly undiscernible as to be beyond analysis. It bears mention, though, that those who never "rejected" (Fr. Davis' chosen word) the Church, but were driven out of her, continued to cling to the common sacramental life of the faithful. It is reported that Döllinger had been accustomed to say mass daily[10] — a contradiction of the priggish Cardinal Vaughan's post-1871 recollections;[11] Tyrrell kept trying to get permission to say mass after his suspension;[12] and as late as 1906, even Loisy asked for the renewal of his permission to celebrate in his own home.[13] (In passing, one is entitled to inquire by what right ecclesiastical authority can forbid a priest to celebrate or a layman to communicate.)

What then would seem to be most needed in warding off lapses is a sense of one's common humanity — and concomitantly,

---

[8] Typical would be the Irish bishop, MacHale, recollecting a meeting with de Lamennais in 1832: "Fortunately for M. De La Mennais he was then accompanied by two young friends who loved him much, but who loved truth and religion more." Ulrick J. Canon Bourke, *The Life and Times of Most Rev. John MacHale* (New York, 1883), p. 96. Similarly, "Laberthonnière never lost his faith and remained faithful to the Church, while Loisy was an apostate who often minimized, contaminated and defamed the subject of his criticism." Jean-Paul Gélinas, *The Revival of Thomism under Leo XIII and The New Philosophies* (Washington, 1959), p. 67. With reference to de Lamennais and Loisy, among others, the Introduction speaks of, "The pride and sufficiency of certain minds had reached, in the middle of the past century, an extreme degree of blindness."

[9] Michael de la Bedoyere, *The Life of Baron von Hügel* (London, 1951), p. 60.

[10] Malcolm MacColl, *Memoirs and Correspondence*, ed. George W. E. Russell (London, 1914), p. 310.

[11] J. G. Snead-Cox, *The Life of Cardinal Vaughan* (St. Louis, 1911), I, p. 64.

[12] De la Bedoyere, *op. cit.*, p. 202.

[13] Alec R. Vidler, *The Modernist Movement in the Roman Church* (Cambridge, 1934), p. 139.

a sense of humor about institutional life, its personages and its appanages. Individual styles are unique, but one does feel that Loisy, too often acerb and brittle, could have benefited by some of the ironic wit of Duchesne — for a while more suspect by Rome than Loisy — who remarked, "I am not a theologian, that is why I can praise God with joy." Or again less whimsically, from Duchesne: "Every year it is for me a lamentable spectacle of an episcopate composed of imbeciles. Our present archbishop is a mitred sacristan"[14] — a comment reminiscent of Newman's reference to Ward, Vaughan, and Manning as "the three tailors of Tooley Street."[15] Perhaps even a touch of curial pragmatism would not be a bad disposition to cultivate, as Archbishop Seton, long America's most decorative prelate at the Quirinal, exemplified: "Theologians make difficulties and canonists get around them."[16] It was at Rome, one recalls, that von Hügel was advised, "Never ask for an *imprimatur*, it is the first step to the *Index*."[17] And when Archbishop Errington was dismissed to the Isle of Man, where he ministered for the remainder of his life as a parish priest, he sardonically noted that "it is not the Holy Ghost that governs the Church, but Msgr. Talbot"[18] — who subsequently was confined to an asylum. More pertinently one might think of the contemporary theologian's *mot* about the contraception decision being held up until the Vatican can get some pharmaceutical stocks into its portfolio.

One must not criticize Fr. Davis for not being somebody else, but one wonders about the pretentious high seriousness of asserting of *Mysterium fidei*: "I should not have accepted the document as a piece of work from a student," just as one wonders about the hardy *contra-mundum* stance in assaulting a nineteenth-century conception of "papal primacy and infallibility." After all, encyclicals come and go, and what one Council has done another can undo. Is not this what we mean by living in history? There is a

[14] De la Bedoyere, op. cit., p. 49.

[15] Maisie Ward, *Insurrection versus Resurrection* (New York, 1937), p. 351.

[16] Archbishop Seton, *Memories of Many Years*, ed. Shane Leslie (New York, 1923), p. 151.

[17] De la Bedoyere, op. cit., p. 49.

[18] Leslie, *Henry Edward Manning*, p. 158.

peculiar strain of "venial egotism"[19] in Fr. Davis' observations: "An imperative urge within me to think creatively has been blocked and stifled beyond endurance by conformity to a rigidly dogmatic Church. . . . I have had to remove a mountain of ecclesiastical rubble in order to produce a few tiny plants of creative thought." Indeed. But have not innovators in every order and way of life had to suffer for their novelties; is not every institution subject to the same laws, the same defects? In the above quotations one glimpses again an indifference to that Leitmotiv of Newman's life which so effectively preserved his spiritual balance: "Now the Church is a Church Militant, and, as the commander of an army is despotic, so must the visible head of the Church be; and therefore *in its idea* the Pope's jurisdiction can hardly be limited"[20] (italics added). But of course, in its execution it will invariably be limited, as will, by definition, any idea be limited in its temporal unfolding. It is the interplay between the "idea" and the "limit" — the latter being an accompaniment and a correlative of the "idea" — which makes for the dynamic tension that constitutes every living institution, and above all that constitutes the viable paradox of the institution which is denominated "the mystical body." Fr. Davis would dissolve the paradox by destroying one pole of its tension: quite literally this is to play the "slacker."

Fortunately we have other models to look upon. Immediately there comes to mind Fr. DuBay who, whatever may be said of his methods, *refuses* to be de-institutionalized, who is acting institutionally — there is no other way — as a limit on an otherwise despotic authority. Fr. Davis bemoans such despotism: "The effort to confine my thinking within the rigid framework of present orthodoxy might in any case have proved too great for me. . . . the official Church no longer for me represents a common thought; it has become a narrow system imposed by authority often against the genuine advance of thought within the Church itself." The sentiments are not new: "Now, if I, as a private priest, put anything into print, Propaganda answers me at once. How can I fight with such a chain on my arm? It is like the

---

[19] The phrase is Vaughan's of Newman's *Apologia*: "The egotism may be disgusting but it is venial." Snead-Cox, *op. cit.*, p. 215.
[20] Wilfrid Ward, *op. cit.*, II, p. 223.

Persians driven to fight under the lash. There was true private judgment in the primitive and medieval schools, — there are no schools now, no private judgment (in the religious sense of the phrase), no freedom, that is, of opinion. That is, no exercise of the intellect. No, the system goes on by the tradition of the intellect of former times."[21] But Newman, shelved at Birmingham and under a cloud[22] far denser than any ever hovering above Fr. Davis, added immediately: "This is a way of things which, in God's own time, will work its own cure, of necessity; nor need we fret under a state of things, much as we may feel it, which is incomparably less painful than the state of the Church before Hildebrand, and again in the fifteenth century."[23] So, to a sense of the totality, and to a sense of humor, we must add a sense of providence, a sense that "truth defends itself, and falsehood refutes itself." And Newman continued: ". . . and that having said my say, time will decide for me, without my trouble, how far it was true, and how far not true."[24] It was of Newman, one of the "kings of modern thought," that Arnold was undoubtedly thinking when he wrote:

> Silent they are, though not content,
> And await to see the future come.
> They have the grief man had of yore,
> But they contend and cry no more.[25]

In fact the "cure" of which Newman wrote is being worked in our own time, as the following would instance. It is now known that Fr. Davis' archbishop had expressed some reservations about material being published in *The Clergy Review* — even as Newman's bishop had had reservations about the *Rambler* under Newman's short-lived editorship. But to Newman's request for a board

[21] *Ibid.*, I, p. 588.

[22] "There he is almost alone in a large house with none of his old friends about him, overworked, and that in a way which is not his own line — not what he had expected or planned for himself or for which he seemed fitted, thrown away by the communion to which he has devoted himself, and evidently sensible that he is so thrown away." *Letters of Frederick Lord Blachford* [Frederick Rogers], ed. George Eden Marinden (London, 1896), p. 96.

[23] *Loc. cit.*

[24] Henry Parry Liddon, D.D., *Life of Edward Bouverie Pusey* (London, 1897), IV, pp. 106–107.

[25] "Stanzas from the Grande Chartreuse."

of censors for the magazine, the bishop's response was simply to bid Newman "to give it up."[26] Whereas in Fr. Davis' case, the January *Clergy Review* noted that after the Archbishop had voiced his concern, "Fr. Davis immediately sent us his resignation, but after further discussion with us and at the personal request of the Archbishop he withdrew it. A *modus vivendi* apparently satisfactory to all parties was reached, whereby Fr. Davis submitted his own choice of priests with pastoral as well as theological knowledge from whom a board of editorial advisors could be nominated. . . ." Plus ça change . . . is not the title of this chapter of church history.[27]

Not only does the nineteenth-century offer some striking contrasts to the twentieth, it also offers some rich examples of how men under great personal pressure responded to ecclesiastical authority, how they parried its blows, temporized, feinted, struck back, or maintained silence; in sum how they expressed in their actions the realization that every institution is a "political" institution. Thus after Bishop Ullathorne's visitation to Newman, bidding him give up the *Rambler*, he published his famous essay, "On consulting the Faithful in Matters of Doctrine"; this was the advantageous moment to strike back, not at Ullathorne but at the system. At other times Newman published under pseudonyms on similar themes; on other more provocative occasions he governed

---

[26] Wilfrid Ward, *op. cit.*, I, p. 497.

[27] That the "cure" is being worked is evident in the present British Apostolic Delegate's response to Herbert McCabe's *New Blackfriars'* editorial for February, 1967, in which Fr. McCabe, after remarking that "The Church is quite plainly corrupt," went on to instance: "A Cardinal selects Christmas as the occasion for supporting the murder of Vietnamese civilians. . . ." The Delegate replied in an interview for the *Catholic Herald* (February 9) that Fr. McCabe took no notice "of the hundreds of bishops who spoke up against one Cardinal who, regrettably let himself be carried away by his emotions as Ordinary Military. . . . " The Delegate's witness became a bit blurred in his subsequent remarks, but the original statement remains undiluted. It should be added that the other examples Fr. McCabe proffers of plain corruption are less cogent than his attack on Spellman, are grossly hyperbolic, or just plain trivial. Equally open to criticism is Fr. McCabe's comment that, "If this Church cannot contain her foremost theologian (and only a quite special theological ignorance and frivolity could see him as 'lightweight') then we must look again very hard both at the Church and at the theology." Mere common sense would dictate that we should look equally hard at Fr. Davis and his views.

himself by the principle, "There are truths that are inexpedient,"[28] and remained silent. Fr. Davis would perhaps characterize these apparent concessions to principle, these maneuvers and tactical deployments, as beneath his dignity as an intellectual. After decrying the fact that "doctrinal declarations [are] won by maneuvering," he adds: "But I was never much interested in palace politics; my life dedication is to faith and theology." The great leaders of the nineteenth-century Catholic enlightenment knew that "faith and theology" must employ "palace politics," that there is an unremitting tension between mystique and politique, and one cannot dispense with either without dispensing ultimately with both.

One might learn other lessons in the maintenance of this tension from the politic response to Roman exorbitance or intransigence made by such theologians as Döllinger or de Lamennais. Döllinger himself told Gregorovius that he had written *Janus* anonymously in order not to sever himself from the Roman communion;[29] one should recall as well the "appeals to Rome" that flowed incessantly, *in propria persona*, anonymously, or pseudonymously, from the pen of de Lamennais. Is it "palace politics" to exercise restraint, to abide by the signs of the time, to have faith in history, to say, for example, as did Döllinger to Newman: "Is it at all prudent, advisable, to write . . . and to try to shake prejudices which seem so firmly rooted?"[30] Such men as Döllinger and de Lamennais did not "reject" the Church, they were hounded out of it; and even then, as when the piteous cry broke from Döllinger, "*Je suis isolé*,"[31] they refused to accept the sentence of Rome. Up to his death Döllinger protested himself a Roman Catholic, and de Lamennais — as Wilfrid Ward accurately observed[32] — finally broke only under the personal harassment of the bishops; and this after nearly a decade of incessant persecution.

We rightly regard such men as our precursors. We regard Dr. Döllinger's *Lectures on the Reunion of the Churches* as a primer

---

[28] Wilfrid Ward, *op. cit.*, II, p. 299.
[29] *The Roman Journals of Ferdinand Gregorovius* (London, 1911), p. 339.
[30] Wilfrid Ward, *op. cit.*, I, p. 493.
[31] Butler, *The Vatican Council*, II, p. 185.
[32] Maisie Ward, *The Wilfrid Wards and the Transition*, p. 317.

of ecumenism for our time as for his own;[33] we applaud de Lamennais for his stimulus to creative theology,[34] and we read the following statement by him as the direct antecedent of *Gaudium et spes*:[35]

Our cause is that of Catholicism, that of the Church, inseparable in itself from the cause of society. To defend the Church and work to revivify its antiquated character [*antique vie*], for too long a time enervated, is therefore to defend society and work for the salvation of people who everywhere today are so suffering that one does not know where to find in preceding centuries, a misery comparable to their misery. . . . The whole of humanity bursts out in a great cry of anguish and is forced to give birth to a new order [*ordre nouveau*]. . . . But, I repeat, the life of nations, principally in the present age, can only be the life of Catholicism, the life of the Church. It is therefore the Church that it is necessary to scrutinize first, it is for its evils that it is necessary to strive to find a remedy for there are no evils that do not derive from hers.

One understands, then, why Newman could reverse his reactionary Anglican opinion of de Lamennais,[36] and three decades later, reading the signs of the time more clearly than Gregory XVI's successors, could declare: "Perhaps La Mennais will be a true prophet after all."[37] One understands, too, why Newman in his declining years, though he was unsympathetic with Döllinger's position, wanted to minister to his spiritual needs. Both outcasts, Döllinger and de Lamennais, were priests who clung to the faith of the Church and looked to history for their vindication. Like Teilhard in our own day, history has proved them prophets.

Perhaps Fr. Davis is also such a prophet. It is not impossible.

---

[33] London, 1872.

[34] "In general one is not able to deny, as we see it, that the School of La Chenaie [de Lamennais' retreat], not only by its example and its exhortations, but by the very questions that it raised, has been one of the factors, and perhaps the most effective at this time, of a renewal in theological speculation." Edgar Hocédez, *Histoire de la Théologie au XIXᵉ Siècle* (Brussels, 1948), I, p. 123.

[35] *Des Maux de l'Église et de Société: Oeuvres complètes de F. de La Mennais* (Paris, 1836–1837), XII, pp. 201–202.

[36] John Henry Cardinal Newman, *loc. cit.*, p. 157. Of de Lamennais, Newman wrote: "Hence he is able to draw close to the democratical party of the day, in that very point in which they most resemble antichrist; and by a strange combination takes for the motto of his *L'Avenir*, 'Dieu et la Liberté.'"

[37] *Unpublished Letters of Matthew Arnold* (New Haven, 1923), p. 60.

Yet there are some indications to the contrary, for, as we have noted, there is lacking to his *apologia* any awareness that the underside of mystique is politique. Nor has he been driven out of the sacramental community but has repudiated it *tout court* in a rant that is both embarrassingly self-revealing and utterly un-just. For if the Church *is* as Fr. Davis envisions it — victim of "collective neurosis," "pathological," "racked by fear, insecurity and anxiety," "intolerant," and "lacking in love" — his is not an idiosyncratic act due to "his own personal make-up," but an act that we are all morally obligated to imitate; for if the Church *is* as Fr. Davis envisions it, it is not the Church at all.

The office for which Fr. Davis has ordained himself presum-ably will be that of prophet of a de-institutionalized Church:

My experience has removed the credibility for me of the official Church as the mode of Christian presence in the world. The Church of Christ is essentially the visibility of grace, namely, the visible model and witness of that interpersonal communion amongst men which is the gift of salvation. By essence the Christian Church has to be the model of human relationships and human community. When I see the official Church in its structure and activity as de-structive of genuine human relationships, I can no longer accept it as the embodiment of grace. Hence I now look for the Church in the more informal groupings of Christians, both within and without the institutional Church, where I find a witness that is credibly Christian.

Alas that the prophetic utterance is so muted and garbled. It is simply too much to ask of any "official" body, of any institution, no matter how perfectly structured and purely administered, that it be "the model of human relationships and human com-munity." The ecclesiastical structure is merely the framework in which community can occur; that the structure may inhibit some people some time is undeniable; but one must assess their anguish in the light of other undeniable benefits the institutional Church does confer — and as a matter of simple intelligence one must question whether this anguish may not often be of their own making, born of hypertrophied idealism.

Any understanding even of smaller communities in the Church, in which the members are bound together by a common work, by a common mode of life, by a common place of residence, that is, any understanding of the workings of religious orders and in-

stitutes elicits as primary datum that even within such communities, lesser communities will invariably be formed of like-
minded and like-spirited persons. It is sheer *Sehnsucht* to imagine
that in any large grouping of individuals one is going to have a
"model of human relationships": the intellectuals will constitute
one such model, the activists another, the devotional another,
the philistines another, all against the backdrop of a larger and less
closely knit community (the religious congregation), which itself
exists against the backdrop of the institutionalized Church. Fr.
Davis with his quest for "models" and abhorrence of "systems"
will just have to learn from another nineteenth-century thinker
"that the true system was something much more complex and
many-sided than I had previously had any idea of, and that its
office was to supply, not a set of model institutions, but principles
from which the institutions suitable to any given circumstances
might be deduced."[38] The lesser components exist in a relationship of reciprocal and creative friction both with one another
and with the larger system, as, for example the Catholic Worker
movement, Friendship House, etc. It smacks of catharism to
assume that only pure communities of committed communicants
should make up a worldwide Church. The *Ecce quam bonum*
has always had a hollow ring when sung by massed choirs.

Fr. Davis notes of the people whom he admires and loves in the
Church: "They do not seem to draw upon the official Church
for the personal and community values they cherish and promote."
Possibly not, but the celebration of the Eucharist would seem
to be a value they do draw upon. And perhaps there are other
values in religion than those pop psychology describes as "interpersonal relationships." For the institutional Church by the very
fact of being a worldly body active in the world has an impact
on worldly men that the purest independent sects do not. If, for
instance, any religious voice is going to make itself listened to in
condemnation of the atrocities of Vietnam, it will not be the
voice of the new cathari — nor even, regrettably, of the Quakers
— but the voice of that supreme pontiff whose "Roman claims"
fill Fr. Davis with "revulsion." That that voice has too often been
silent when one would have liked to hear it speak forthrightly

---

[38] John Stuart Mill, *Autobiography*, ed. Currin V. Shields (New York,
1957), p. 104.

is all the more reason for not conspiring to muffle it altogether. The powers of this world are influenced only by worldly — that is, by institutionalized — power. It was only because the dissenters of Clapham were organized under the leadership of Wilberforce and because he himself joined the highest religious motives to directly political action that the abolition of slavery was achieved. The Old Catholic movement "has come to nothing,"[39] wrote that entirely worldly observer, Jowett, when he saw that the movement could exercise no effective power. Nor did Stalin mockingly ask: How many divisions have the Italian sects?

Moreover, the institution provides channels of communication and action that are already existent. It provides the instruments for reform, however blunt and bent those instruments from time to time may be. Undoubtedly, as Rosemary Ruether has so frequently noted, we are moving towards a more fluid structure within the Church, a structure in which the old frameworks of parish and diocese, of geography and time, of narrow confessional allegiance and affiliation, may be dissolved, in which greater dissent and more evangelical witnessing will be the norm — but always, as Dr. Ruether has brilliantly emphasized,[40] against the backdrop of a common tradition and ideal, a tradition and ideal which by reason of its very universality must inevitably be incarnated in its own structure, in its own "institution." Institutions are not the lengthened shadows of men, but of ideas, ideas which must become institutionalized if they are to become realities.

The Protestant moralist, Paul Ramsey, perhaps too conscious of the truth in the above generalities, has often accused certain pacifists like Gordon Zahn of being sectaries because, it is alleged, in the interest of purity of doctrine they would diminish the Church's influence on secular affairs.[41] The accusation is founded on a faulty ecclesiology which does not take sufficiently into account that, as Congar said, "Il faut, dans l'Église, des prophètes";[42] for the prophet is merely the providential instrument

---

[39] *Letters of Benjamin Jowett*, ed. Evelyn Abbott and Lewis Campbell (New York, 1899), p. 76.

[40] "Post-Ecumenical Christianity," *The Ecumenist*, V, 1.

[41] " . . . the fact is that Zahn is a sectarian." *Cross Currents* (Fall, 1963); for other documentation and critique see Lawler, *op. cit.*, p. 69.

[42] *Vraie et fausse Réforme dans l'Église*, pp. 169 ff.

to guarantee that in the Church the means do not obscure or defile the ends. The prophet, then, is as necessary as the adminis-trator — but not much more than that. Moreover, the accusation is baseless because the sectary, by definition, cuts himself off from the Church. It is not the peace agitators, the civil-rights rebels, the theological renovators, the institutional goads who have lost sight of the dialectic tension that exists within the Christian community, as within every other human organization, it is those who like Fr. Davis explicitly and formally "reject" one of the sus-taining poles of that tension. That there are bishops and func-tionaries — Roman "lackeys" as Newman termed them — who would reject the other pole makes neither them nor Fr. Davis less blameworthy.

The parallel to Fr. Davis, therefore, is not Dr. Döllinger, Abbé de Lamennais, or Cardinal Newman. The parallel, sadly, must be drawn from more recent days and is with Abbé Jean Massin and his Community of Christian Hope. Abbé Massin wrote (though in the days of Humani generis and of the condemnation of the worker priests, and therefore patently less unjustifiably than Davis) :[43]

The Community of Christian Hope is composed of men and women united together in order to seek to live and to think along the lines of a truly evangelical Christianity which shall respond to the needs and values of our epoch, and which will be able to give some meaning to the daily lives of our contemporaries. The Community does not want to become a new sect. We wish to maintain a bond of fra-ternal union with all the men of our age whose religious unrest has not been allayed elsewhere, and who want to live with Jesus. . . . It is in conjugal love that God aids us to understand how He wishes to unite Himself to humanity and to each man. . . . The Community of Christian Hope rejects any moral doctrine, whatever it may be, which makes the idolatrous pretension of codifying an imitation of Jesus Christ. . . . Can I believe at once in Jesus and in Rome?

In the past decade and a half nothing more has been heard of Abbé Massin and his group.

One final historical parallel may be allowed. Alexander Dru in

---

[43] From mimeographed materials privately circulated. Commentaries on the group may be found in Informations Catholiques (February 14, 1952); La Vie Intellectuelle (February, 1952); Life of the Spirit (March, 1952); and in Massin's book, Le Festin chez Lévi (Paris, 1952).

a characteristically brilliant study, *Erneurung und Reaktion: Die Restauration in Frankreich 1800–1830*, notes that de Lamennais had long been exalted by Sainte-Beuve as another Pascal. But of de Lamennais the defector, Sainte-Beuve wrote:

What forgetfulness! . . . How is it possible to abdicate on a sudden in such a way? Is it permissible? Nothing could be worse, let me tell you, than to provoke faith in other souls and to move like that à *l'improviste*, leaving them high and dry. Nothing is so calculated to throw them into the scepticism which you still deplore, though you have nothing that is not vague to put in its place. How many souls have I known whom you held and carried in your pilgrim's haversack, and when that haversack was dumped on the ground were left lying in the ditch! Public opinion, the voice of flattery, new souls such as are always attracted by genius will no doubt console you and make it possible to forget; but though my cry should sound like a lament, I shall denounce your forgetfulness![44]

"Brutal," as Dru rightly notes. Brutal, but perhaps accurate, above all in the light of Davis' own book defending his apostasy, *A Question of Conscience*[45] — a brief examination of which will close this discussion.

The historian, James Anthony Froude, disciple of both Newman and Carlyle, noted in his memoirs that these were the only two intellectual giants of the era — a judgment Carlyle did his bit to cancel out by opining that Newman had not "the intellect of a moderate-sized rabbit."[46] It may not, therefore, appear too unseemly if, acting on such historical precedent, and making due allowance for the clearly differing magnitudes, the present writer opines that Charles Davis — as all the preceding implies — is theologically very small beer — a judgment hardly to be confuted by Davis' *apologia*.

A Question of Conscience is a book, inept, pretentious, and trite: trite, because it is only another contribution to a whole genre of ex-Catholic tracts all invariably detailing the same bases for defecting: suppression of personal rights, formalism, corruption, and (without fail) papal infallibility — of which Newman noted that, while he didn't like it, it would probably make very little

---

[44] Munich, 1966, p. 134.

[45] New York, 1967.

[46] James Anthony Froude, *Thomas Carlyle: A History of His Life in London* (London, 1885), II, p. 247.

difference in the practical order: and it hasn't. Davis' charges are serious, and should be taken seriously; but they constitute a case to be proved, not, as he seems to feel, an a priori to be explicitated. The book is pretentious because great gobs of intellectual flab are bound up in some strained theological exercises. The book is inept because its effort at exposition of intimate personal relations takes the form of a dumfounding woodenness, of which one example more than suffices: "Florence is very much an individual person, with her own distinctive background and temperament, with her own qualities of mind and heart, with her own medical history and physical makeup" (p. 32). Though there is a good deal of discussion of the whole marital matter, nothing need be observed here, except, with Rupert Brooke, that

> . . . there are
> Meads from Haslingfield to Coton
> Where *das Betreten's* not *Verboten*.[47]

It is the theological argument alone that one can judge. We begin with some quotations (italics supplied throughout):

To argue that the Church in its existing structure and life is *of itself a sign sufficient for faith* comes to asserting this: the Church is the visible embodiment of Christian faith, hope and love, and as such draws men to itself (p. 62).

In other words, the Church of Christ is of its essence the *visible embodiment* of the truth and love of Christ, retaining sufficient signs of its credibility in that respect (p. 182).

The Church, it is argued, is a perennial sign of its own divine origin. By its universal unity, by the sublimity and holiness of its teaching and by the *inexhaustible fruitfulness of the Christian life within it*, it manifests that it comes from God and forms of itself a sufficient motive of credibility to lead men to faith and to sustain the faith of its members (p. 61).

The Church remains apostolic by preserving and fostering the faith of the apostles and by being like the apostolic community *an embodiment of Christian hope and love* (p. 63).

We consider the last quotation first and appraise it against the screen of a portrait of the existing Church which, for Charles Davis, so visibly fails to embody the virtues of the apostolic community. The portrait is not pleasing: money intended for the

---

[47] "The Old Vicarage, Grantchester."

poor is diverted to the private gain of churchmen; the most vicious social abuses are benignly tolerated; women are demeaned as inferiors; a widespread acceptance of discrimination reduces many people, even church members, to a chattle state; bishops denounce other bishops; services of worship have been known to degenerate into orgies of sexual license; ecclesiastical functionaries boast of the great sums they have sent abroad to prop up the enfeebled mother Church; the whole life of the intellect, and particularly philosophy, is decried; factions favoring traditional ways and factions favoring updating sow hatred among ordinary Christians; superstition is rampant; pious rhetorical formulae abound; churchmen advocate submission to the established political order; reports are heard from all sides of contention, envy, animosity, dissension, detraction, gossip, and arrogance. In short, disorder reigns.

There are exceptions to this grim picture — and Charles Davis concedes them — but basically this is what we face; one must almost join Davis in his anguishing over how unlike all this is to "the apostolic community as an embodiment of Christian hope and love." And one must almost conclude with him that, if "the Church in its existing structure and life is of itself a sign sufficient for faith," undeniably this institution, *this* conflict-wracked, divided, and manifestly corrupt community is not such a sign, is not therefore the true Church of Christ.

The argument cannot be faulted. Regrettably, one has to conclude there must be something wrong with its premises, since this entire portrait was drawn from the Acts and from St. Paul: this Church we have been describing *is* the Apostolic Church.

This raises some questions — mainly about how we are to read the signs of the Church as well as of the times — that we shall look at in a moment, but first, some additional historical problems. Charles Davis sets great store in "visible embodment," as we have seen. But any reading of history, even by the most bigoted anti-Christian or anti-Romanist, makes clear that the state of the present Church is purer than the Church at the end of the Dark Ages, purer than during the Babylonian Captivity, purer than during the high Renaissance, purer than during the reign of Pio Nono. And even the most prejudiced historian would have to say that the evils embodied in the Church have been less apparent as each new age dawned, so that what would have been tolerated during the reign of Leo X would have been abominated during the reign of Pius IX, and what was tolerated during the reign of Pius IX was in fact abominated by John XXIII. The question, then, is where was the visible embodiment of love and holiness during those preceding periods when corruption was so much more rampant than subsequently. According to Charles Davis if that visible embodiment is not evident, neither is the true Church present. In this case for hundreds of years in the past the true Church was non-existent, and any existing Church today has lost continuity with that apostolic Church — which itself did not appear very visibly "true." Nor can one take refuge from this dilemma, as Davis attempts to do, by saying that earlier "institutional structures" were open to reform while those of today are not. Institutional structures are not visible embodiments; we only know structures by *what* is structured, that is, by the displayed holiness or corruption that they engender or enforce.

The explanation of all this is that Charles Davis is theologically a materialist — not, of course, in any gross sense, but in the sense of being a naïve literalist. This materialism leads to a defective theory of sign, of credibility, and of "embodiment." As to the first, the signs, or "notes," of the Church are not proofs; they are what they profess to be, "signs" — if they were anything more, all men would be compelled to assent to them and be open automatically, mechanically even, to the gift of Faith. Every sign by definition obscures as it clarifies and no sign unequivocally signifies the same reality to everybody.

Second, as to the "traditional understanding of faith and credibility" (p. 179), on which Davis professes to depend, it must be noted that it is a tradition not honored anywhere today. Moreover, his implicit notion of *assensus necessarius* leading to *cognitio certa*, and reducing the act of Faith to a kind of syllogism never entered the central stream of traditional theology. While it is possible that one individual note of the Church — in this case, holiness — may be a sufficient motive of credibility, in no specific instance need this in fact be so. Newman, with his radical awareness of the omnigenous character of the elements leading to assent, developed a doctrine of the "convergence of probabilities" to explain precisely this multiform character of the preludes to

belief. Credibility is posited, in the actual order of human understanding, not by the mental machine Charles Davis has designed
but by something infinitely more flexible, polymorphic, ambiguous, supple. Traditionally this "something" has been denominated "spirit."

Lastly, there is Davis' defective notion of "embodiment." Prescinding from what has been said above, one would have to follow
him out of the Roman Catholic communion if one embraced
his line of reasoning: holiness is a visible note of the true Church.
The following quotation elaborates the logic:

> The Church is a community of men who remain subject to sin and
> error. It is rightly said to be a human community. We should not
> be surprised to find it a Church of sinners and as a social body, not
> just in its individual members, marred by many defects and failings.
> Our relation with the Church has therefore to be discriminating.
> Not all that is of the Church is of Christ or of God.

> But as the Church of Christ, the community of Christians, despite all
> sin and failure, essentially remains the visible presence of Christ.
> In other words, the Church of Christ is of its essence the visible
> embodiment of the truth and love of Christ, retaining sufficient signs
> of its credibility in that respect. Only thus can it mediate faith in
> Christ to men and continue to serve as the embodiment of Christ's
> presence in the world (p. 182).

Undergirding this apparently rigorous theological reasoning is the
same materialism encountered above which would make visibility
of holiness ultimately and necessarily dependent on a sociologist's
survey, on a numerical, or otherwise measurable, poll determining separation of sheep from goats. The Church of Christ, then,
is to be adjudged by statisticians, with Dr. Gallup alone pos-
sessing what used to be called "the discernment of spirit" — and
which now must be called the discernment of NORC. Would
that it were that clear. Though, were it that clear, perhaps mankind would have flocked to synagogue or stoa rather than to the
wrangling, haggling, and wracked apostolic Church; and we today
might all convert to Buddhism.

One can no more imagine that to be the case, than one can
imagine any theologian maintaining with Charles Davis that
Roman Catholicism "imposes as a condition for membership
belief in its social structure as of divine institution." The visible
embodiment of the Church's holiness is not to be determined

by counting the good people in it, though that may be for some an important "sign." It is simply astonishing that a professor who himself tells us that he "was regarded as the leading Roman Catholic theologian in Great Britain" (p. 5), a professor above all of *sacramental* theology — it is simply astonishing that such a theologian would have ignored so completely the fact that the visible embodiment of the Church's holiness is in her sacraments. *This* is the sign that the Church holds before "the nations." One must ask: "Art thou a master in Israel and dost not know these things?"

What the defection of Charles Davis comes down to, then, must be either the result of personal factors involved in his celibacy-marriage difficulties — which are nobody's business but his — or the result of some non-rational, and thus indiscussible conviction that Roman Catholicism is intrinsically and essentially irreformable. Throughout the book the refrain recurs: John XXIII was an exception; liberal theologians though in good grace with authority are exceptions; present-day Dutch and American open-Catholicism is an exception. Behind this is the belief that the reform of Catholicism from Leo XIII on is an exception, that the reform of Catholicism from the Reformation on was an exception, that the reform of Catholicism from the Council of Constance on was an exception, that the reform of Catholicism from Hildebrand on was an exception. Ultimately the Incarnation is an exception, history is an exception. At this point the circle closes; Charles Davis is correct. Spirit *is* an exception.

V

CONTRACEPTION AND THE NATURAL LAW

It is impossible to believe that the unprecedented statement of Pope Paul on birth control (June 23, 1964) was intended to terminate all discussion on this question, though such an interpretation was placed upon it by some secular journalists and some diocesan weeklies. The apparent aim of the Pope's remarks was to foreclose any definitive and in the end embarrassing judgments from being rendered either by individual bishops or by national hierarchies. The statement, then, was a clear recognition of the collegiality of the whole Church, for if the bishops were to restrain themselves from issuing decisions on this question it could only be in order that the theologians and the concerned laity might express themselves more freely and thus bear witness to the beliefs and aspirations of the whole body of the faithful.

American Catholicism, by reason of its popular devotions which are mainly Latin in origin, and its religious communities which are for the most part either Latin or Irish in origin, has always had a strong ultramontanist cast. American theologians, therefore, tend to treat the various allocutions of recent popes, and particularly of Pius XII, much after the manner of the biblical fundamentalist interpreting the sacred text, and they are affronted by such a statement as Newman's that "The Church moves as a whole; it is not a mere philosophy, it is a communion; it not only discovers, but it teaches; it is bound to consult for charity as well as for faith."[1]

Toward the end of his life, Cardinal Newman told the young

---

[1] Wilfrid Ward, *The Life of John Henry Cardinal Newman* (London, 1912), II, p. 296.

Wilfrid Ward that what was most needed for the Church was "fair and candid discussion between the representatives of the specialized sciences and the theologians."[2] Strangely enough, in all the recent furor over the question of contraception, it has been the theologians who seem to have insulated themselves against any "fair and candid discussion." An outsider would almost believe that the Church is not made up of bishops and laity at all, but only of professors of canon law and moral theology. What Newman said of the ultramontanist bishops at the time of the First Vatican Council is true today of many moralists and canonists: "They have not come into contact with the intellectual mind of the times."[3] And the nineteenth-century bishops, like many contemporary scholastic theologians, could not come into contact with this "intellectual mind" because the laity were not formed to bear open witness to what they believed as well as to the culture in which these beliefs were held.

What Newman was saying in England had been affirmed a few years earlier by his great contemporary, Matthias Joseph Scheeben, and it is as relevant to moral as to dogmatic teaching, and to 1968 as to 1864.[4]

It follows that the public profession of doctrine by the body of the faithful, being a witnessing of the Holy Ghost relatively independent, ought logically and briefly to precede the precise declaration of the teaching body, and in such circumstances influence, as a means of orientation, its future judgment.

But the layman has an obligation not only to testify in union with his pastors to the religious tradition; he has a further obligation to bear witness to all the legitimate longings and aspirations of the faithful. Apart from the question of contraception where the lay voice has been muted, the obvious example of an area in which there has been effective lay witnessing is that of the arts. Two decades ago it was not uncommon to find clerical critics condemning certain realistic works of fiction or of the cinema on premises that were so completely detached from the actual conditions of a Christian living in the twentieth century that these condemnations often had little effect other than to

[2] *Ibid.*, II, p. 468.
[3] Cuthbert Butler, O.S.B., *The Vatican Council* (London, 1930), II, p. 29.
[4] *Dogmatik* (Freiburg, 1948), Sect. 14, 99.

lead to a disregard for authority itself. Concerning the arts for example, a moralist can rarely justify defining occasions of sin simply on the basis of abstract principles and his own personal response to this or that artifact. Rather, what would be required is a profound knowledge, certainly of theology, but also of esthetics, of the social structure of various groups, of the psychology of attention, and of a host of other factors which generally come within the scope of specialized lay research.

Should an occasional theologian be found conversant and capable in all these fields, there will probably yet be lacking to him that empathic awareness of conditions in the large body of the faithful which the layman possesses, as it were, connaturally. And if this can be maintained of so relatively public an area as that of the arts how much more nearly true must it be of the whole domain of sexuality where not only modesty but prudery and a score of other inhibiting influences prevent any easy understanding — above all by theologians who are celibates. Moral teachings, as the human though not fallible expressions of the immutable ethical code, are not precisioned in a vacuum, nor even in a confessional, a pulpit, or a lecture hall. They are generated at that point where meditative reason, enlightened by theological wisdom, comes to grips with concrete realities; they are not the product of the isolated mind, nor of the group "mind," but they are defined by the entire Christian community acting as a complete *person*. It might be said that their "body" is given in all its physical and pragmatic richness primarily by the layman; their "mind" is that ordinance of reason which moralists — whether lay or clerical — discern; and their "soul" is the sanction of the bishop which purifies and enforces them. Moreover, since it is the Christian community that defines this teaching, then grace acts both to enlighten and inform it.

Christian moral doctrine, then, is an expression of that collegiality which dogmatic theologians have rediscovered only recently, and which should be characterized by a kind of perichoretic harmony, as among equals. Recent efforts on the part of moral theologians to silence the lay voice are simply Sabellian in intent.

There is an anti-intellectual doctrine known as traditionalism which maintains that man cannot by the power of reason alone come to a knowledge of God's existence or of any absolute truth. The traditionalists or fideists in order to explain the knowledge of a supreme being, therefore, posited some kind of primitive revelation which had been handed down from generation to generation, had been refined by the philosophers and purified by the teaching of the Scriptures and the Church. As we all know, this notion, widely held even into the middle of the last century through the influence of de Lamennais, was condemned definitively by the First Vatican Council in its affirmation that the existence of God is a truth naturally knowable. Traditionalism was in part an expression of that general and not entirely unwholesome denigration of reason which stemmed from the *devotio moderna* and which was consummated in the exaggerated "supernaturalism" of the romantics, whether Catholic or not; but traditionalism was also, paradoxically, an expression of a very reasonable desire to understand the widespread denial of the existence of God in post-Renaissance Europe. For, so the traditionalists argued, if the existence of God is a truth attainable by unaided reason, how can one explain the fact that people, as obviously endowed with reason as any theists, can simply reject all arguments for his existence. To ascribe such disbelief always and invariably to intellectual or moral perversity was in effect to question the honesty, sincerity, and intelligence of great numbers of people who appeared to be no less gifted with those virtues than any believers.

A similar problem faces those who argue on the ground of natural law against all forms of contraception. It is quite obvious that many people as earnest and as capable of scrutinizing nature and its laws as are the opponents of contraception have not been persuaded by the natural-law argument employed by Catholics. This raises a number of questions concerning the value of a natural teaching that is unattainable by human nature which I shall consider in a moment. But, first, one must inquire as to the origin of the notion that contraception is intrinsically immoral. Only three solutions would seem to be possible for this problem. Either the teaching on the immorality of contraception is part of revelation, in which case one must determine its source; or it was a conclusion reasoned to by the creators of the now traditional view, in which case one must determine why reasons cogent in the past are no longer cogent to men of good will in the present; or finally, it was based on certain sociological, cultural, and biological presuppositions which are no longer valid or binding.

There is perhaps a fourth and corollary possibility: that the conclusion, while attainable by reason alone, given the power of concupiscence was in fact rarely attained, and that therefore the light of faith was required to illuminate the teaching. There are, as we know, certain natural truths, even in the physical order, that can be known with certitude only through faith: thus the implications of the doctrine of the Immaculate Conception seem to have made it fairly clear that a human person comes into being only when the fused sperm and egg, the gamete, are capable of further cell division. This is quite a different teaching from the old scholastic view that a person exists only after the vegetative and sensitive soul have been subsumed in a rational soul, a process which was believed to occur some months after what we know as mitosis; it is also quite a different teaching from that of Anglo-Saxon jurisprudence which allows human rights only to a viable fetus. But though these radical discrepancies between canon law and civil law, and between a position not universally accepted — at least in theory — before 1854 and the subsequent position which is implicitly *de fide*, do raise problems regarding the relation of natural law and revelation, these problems are not essentially different from those raised by our first hypothetical answer to the initial question: that is, that the condemnation of contraception as intrinsically immoral is a part of revelation.

Setting aside momentarily all arguments in favor of the official position founded on natural law alone, the basic issue now concerns the role of revelation. There is virtually a unanimous consensus of fathers and doctors throughout the Christian tradition of the past that the condemnation of contraception can be based on the story of Onan in the Old Testament. This consensus of the tradition was reinforced by Pius XI's citation of that same scriptural passage in *Casti Connubii*. Similarly, it is a unanimous consensus of fathers and doctors, and of acts of the ordinary magisterium, which has led contemporary theologians to view the present teaching as irrevocable. However, as has been pointed out frequently in current discussions of the questions, there are large numbers of biblical scholars today who do not believe that the punishment of Onan has any bearing on the matter of contraception as such. Unfortunately, what has been overlooked with regard to this last fact is not merely that if the consensus of theological opinion is no longer unanimous in finding the story of Onan as a revealed source of the condemnation, then that unanimous consensus which resulted in condemning contraception on those grounds is dissolved, but also that if unanimous consensus is the indispensable note of an irrevocable teaching, then obviously we are going to have to revise our ideas of unanimous consensus. For what was a unanimous consensus in the case of the interpretation of the story of Onan over the last fifteen hundred years, and what was therefore believed irrevocably taught, is no longer unanimous, and the interpetation has been generally revoked. The same may certainly be true in the case of contraception as such, above all when the revealed basis for the condemnation has been shown to be very possibly non-existent. May it not theoretically be, then, that there can be no such thing as an irrevocably binding unanimous consensus of the theological school and of the ordinary teaching of the magisterium until true unanimity has been attained, that is, until the end of time?

If the immorality of contraception is not explicitly revealed, yet, it has been suggested, it may be implicitly revealed in St. Paul's condemnation of homosexuality and other perversions. Thus Fathers Kelly and Ford observe:[5]

> But might not St. Paul's repudiation of one or several unnatural sex practices be taken to include implicitly a condemnation of other unnatural sex practices that are not mentioned explicitly? If such an interpretation is correct, then the immorality of at least some forms of contraception (*coitus interruptus* and condomistic intercourse) would be implicitly revealed.

But with regard to condomistic intercourse it is very difficult to see how such an interpretation could ever be correct, since it is based on a patent begging of the question. What we are seeking is to determine if the immorality of contraception has been revealed; we cannot rely on arguments based on natural law alone, since these arguments are not cogent; nor can we rely

---

[5] John C. Ford, S.J., and Gerald Kelly, S.J., *Contemporary Moral Theology* (Westminster, 1963), II, p. 272.

on a consensus of the school because this consensus is based on
a seriously flawed scriptural interpretation. Obviously, if the question were only of homosexuality, or probably were only of *coitus
interruptus*, one could invoke St. Paul in proof of this confirmation
of natural law by revelation, since homosexuality, and probably
coitus interruptus whether culpable or not, are also condemned on
the grounds of natural law. What we are seeking ultimately to determine is why theologians believe that contraception is immoral.
The basis for the condemnation must be either reason or revelation or some coalescence of the two. But since reason has proved
unable to yield any such basis it is impossible to stigmatize contraception as unnatural and to group it with various other unnatural practices condemned by St. Paul. For if that were a valid
line of exegesis, why confine it to this passage in St. Paul? Frat-
ricide, incest, and a score of unnatural vices are all condemned
in various places in the Bible, and with this loose canon of interpretation one could take the biblical repudiation of one or
several such unnatural practices as including implicitly a condemnation of every other allegedly unnatural practice that is not
mentioned explicitly. Certainly one may do this: but it offers no
real solution unless one knows antecedently that the "other"
practices which are not explicitly mentioned are really unnatural:
and this is precisely what we don't know, and what we are trying
to determine.

The question remains, therefore, from what source did churchmen derive their condemnation of contraception, if it is neither
explicitly nor implicitly revealed, and if it cannot be certified
clearly and cogently by reason. Fathers Kelly and Ford suggest
as a third possibility that the "entire natural law is implicitly
contained in the two great commandments and the Decalogue."
This argument parallels that in the preceding paragraph, but
since these two distinguished and generally forebearing authors
seem to find it an important proposition, it may be discussed
further. They note that:

> . . . every pope who has distinguished between natural law and
> revealed law was conscious of the fact that some of the natural law
> (e.g. the Decalogue) is explicitly revealed. It seems to us, therefore,
> that the real purpose of such assertions is to vindicate the Church's
> power to teach and to apply the natural law, whether it be revealed

or not. Thus, such papal statements leave open the question whether the natural law is also contained in revelation, at least implicitly.[6]

However, while unquestionably some of the natural law is explicitly revealed, none of it is explicitly revealed qua natural law: the determination of what in revelation relates to natural law can be made only by reason. After it has been determined by reason that something falls under the scope of natural law, the Church may illuminate the identity or similarity between this particular natural law principle and revelation, and such illumination may even enrich our understanding of the original principle, even as christology has enriched the philosophical understanding of the nature of the person. But what is not possible is for the Church globally to legislate that teachings which cannot be verified by reason can be shown by revelation to be verifiable by reason. Nor, as we have seen above, is it possible for the Church to proclaim that an allegedly natural law principle is contained in revelation without also disclosing where in revelation it is explicitly or implicitly contained. Either such disclosure will carry one back to the Scriptures or it will not: if it doesn't, then one will have to assume that there is such a thing as a constitutive tradition, that is, a body of revealed truth which is entirely independent of the biblical revelation. One is free or not to embrace such a concept of tradition, though it flies in the face of a large body of contemporary theological opinion to do so.

The circularity of the arguments used to relate revelation to natural law is again brought out in Kelly and Ford's final statement:[7]

But even if all these possibilities [considered above] were rejected, there would still remain the consideration of whether the entire natural law (and this would include the *immorality of contraception*) is not a secondary object of infallibility because it is intimately connected with revelation. The idea here is that, since supernatural salvation is certainly a part of the depositum fidei, *all the requirements for the attainment of salvation* are intimately connected with the depositum fidei, even though not in themselves revealed. It seems to us that at least in this minimum sense, the *natural law* must be considered an object of infallibility, and that this, as well as the other possibilities explained in this section, should be more thor-

[6] *Ibid.*, p. 274.
[7] *Ibid.*, pp. 274–275.

oughly discussed by the specialists in fundamental theology. It is
our conviction that, whatever be the explanation, there can be no
reasonable doubt that the Church can infallibly interpret the *entire
natural law* (italics added).

All of this presumes that natural law has made it unmistakably
clear that contraception is immoral. There seems to be no awareness when speaking of "all the requirements to salvation" that
there are large numbers of non-Catholic Christians who believe
contraception to be an aid to marital union, and therefore to the
sanctification of themselves and their children. Unless this position can be shown to be a contradiction of the natural law, it is
difficult to see how revelation enters into the discussion here at all.

What is to be noted in the above passage is the peculiar statement: "whatever be the explanation, there can be no reasonable
doubt that the Church can infallibly interpret the entire natural
law." One would have thought that the mode of explanation
would be essential, and that any such explanation would have to
take as its premise that such and such a truth is in fact a determination of natural law. This indifference to explanations is
characteristic of much Catholic writing on contraception, so
that the impression is sometimes given that Catholic theologians
are intent above all on reaching a predetermined conclusion, no
matter what rules of logic may have to be dispensed with en route.[8]

If the condemnation of contraception cannot be based on
natural law, cannot be based on revelation, cannot be based on
ecclesiastical faith — unless one accepts the notion of a constitutive
tradition — one again is compelled to search for its sources. I do
not think it a novel assumption to say that it may well be founded
on certain cultural and sociological factors which have con-

---

[8] The tautology that underlies much argument against contraception is
evident in some highly intemperate remarks, which implicitly deride
the witness of the layman, by John J. Lynch, S.J., who argues against
the liceity of anovulants on the grounds that their use means the temporary
suppression "of the generative function as such, that is, precisely as generative" (*Theological Studies*, June, 1964, p. 241). Unfortunately this kind of
circular logic is not very compelling to most Christians because the very point
at issue is whether this "function" is properly denominated only as "generative." After all, it is by the names of things that we first come to know their
natures and properties, and no one except those inexperienced in precisely
this field refers to intercourse, physical union, coition, copulation, etc. as
the "generative act."

ditioned Catholic theologians and therefore Catholic theology in its course through the centuries. In many cases these factors have influenced the generality of western men as well, but since these comments are centered on a specifically Catholic problem, I will confine myself to some brief instances of what I have elsewhere called the celibate *Denkform*.

It would be impossible to do any kind of justice to this subject in this short essay,[9] as it ranges over such peculiar notions as Justin Martyr's denunciation of the *Iliad* as being concerned with only one thing, "woman,"[10] to the clerical editors of *Sign* magazine condemning Governor Rockefeller after his divorce as unworthy of the presidency, and this notwithstanding the fact that the only other announced candidate had publicly stated that he wanted "a test of strength with the Soviet Union," and that he was "against all disarmament." In general this mindset, which is not confined to clerics, shows a greater preoccupation with personal and individual morality than with social; demeans the place of woman because it sees in her only an instrument for breeding or conversely elevates her to a quasi-deity (where she is safely beyond reach of all cloying human passion); consequently it warps the understanding of sexuality by apotheosizing it (hence the spate of recent naïve clerical works glorifying sexual union) or demeaning it (hence the pre-twentieth-century Augustinian tradition of regarding sex as smirched).

In the clerical and legalistic conception of sexuality the law of charity is sometimes lost sight of entirely, whether it be, for instance, charity in that relationship between spouses which may make the limitation of children through means other than abstinence psychologically, and even physically indispensable, or charity toward priests who have fallen from their state and married. Concerning the latter, whose plight is often ignored, there are the best of grounds for being distressed at the scores of good and godfearing men who for one reason or emotion or another have had to abandon their state, and who have been the victims of an almost systematic social revulsion and reprobation on the part of

[9] I have discussed certain historical influences relating to this theme in "The Christian Understanding of Love," *The Christian Imagination* (Westminster, 1955).

[10] *Discourse to the Greeks*, I (provenance dubious), in Christian Heritage, *St. Justin Martyr* (New York, 1948), p. 432.

Catholics. The religious, to say nothing of the social and economic, condition of these priests is worse than that of Catholics who are divorced and also destined by our moral legislators to live out their lives in a permanent "state of sin," unless they can abandon their legal spouses and families. Certainly if Christ could embrace the Magdalen some accommodations can be made in the name of charity for all these people; but that canon law treats them so severely, can provide them with no solace until their deaths, points up how much more emphasis is placed on sexual union than in fact it deserves to have. It is not necessarily the laity seeking an adaptation of the laws concerning contraception who are preoccupied with sexuality; it may as well be those clergy who cannot see it in its place as only one among many elements determining a man's nature, and who, like Augustine, imagine that if it weren't for the need to copulate Adam would have found a better helpmate in another man.[11]

The present sharp divergence of opinion between great numbers of laity and a majority of the clergy points up how fully Catholicism has been institutionalized around the written word. Given a biblical cult, this focus was almost imperative. But it is enormously exaggerated by the fact that for centuries the only literate people were celibates and the products of a celibate training which itself contained a strong admixture of false asceticism and implicit heresy. As with all such closed cultures the predominantly theological literature which this literacy begot reflects only an intermarriage of congruent and related ideas, and it would be sociologically impossible to expect to extract from it any strong indications of variant views. It is only in the last four centuries — and even more recently for Roman Catholics — that the voices from the underground so long suppressed are now dissolving the hegemony of celibates and clerics (the word clericus itself points up this relationship of literacy and celibacy) and creating a religious literature which includes the worldly and the laic. It is understandably a shock to the theologians to realize that truths which they had so long nurtured, exchanged, and rarified in their debates are regarded by the now-literate masses as fragmentary or simply irrelevant.

---

11 De Genesi ad litteram, IX, 5, 9.

But because in the pre-Renaissance world the lay currents which did find expression in the popular culture were never recognized by the theologians, the result was the same kind of inbreeding of ideas and mores among the masses as among their political and religious overlords. Whenever any stratum of society is cut off from interchange with the other levels the result can only be the kind of cultural monstrosities which in the present instance are evident in the Goliardic literature, in the literature of *l'amour courtois*, and in the Augustinian doctrine on marriage — strictly a doctrine, as a score of events, such as the influx of prostitutes to Constance at the time of the general council or the widespread clerical concubinage, would suggest. It is therefore only in our time that there can be a fruitful dialogue between the celibates, clerics, theologians, and the married, worldly laity.

Sitz im Leben, an important catchphrase in modern biblical exegesis, means that a given scriptural text must be set in the context for which it was written by its human author. The results of this kind of approach to the Bible have been truly revolutionary. Strangely enough, however, while biblical theologians have been willing to apply this critical method to the sacred text, moral theologians have been less liberal in extending it to various opinions of the school or decrees and formulations of the magisterium. Moreover, for the present student of sexuality, it is a question not merely of knowing the disputes that provoked a particular decision of authority, but rather of understanding the whole social ambit in which these disputes occurred. For example, it seems apparent that the doctrine of the primary end of marriage would be considerably more applicable to a society which was devastated by periodic plagues, and which had no knowledge of elementary hygiene or prophylaxis, than to a society such as ours in which the birthrate is outstripping — Colin Clark notwithstanding — the manifest capacities of the economy to create new resources.

Man is not only the passive subject of evolution; he controls it. And it is quite conceivable as he more and more grows in self-awareness, and consequently in the power of directing his own evolution, that the problem of contraception may resolve itself — even to the satisfaction of the theologians. If we are now in a stage of thinking on this problem radically different from that of the nineteenth century when contraception was universally condemned by all major Christian bodies, that is, if we are now in a stage when contraception is seen by many Christians as essential to deepening the interpersonal aspects of marriage, we are entitled by every law of history to forecast a future stage in which sexual love may not be rooted primarily in genital union, but will be incarnated and expressed in other forms. The traditional canonical position may thus be organically reasserted as intercourse will be seen as primarily directed to procreation. For this reason one can accept the conclusion of Paul Chauchard — the great interpreter of the work of Teilhard from the perspective of neurophysiology — that "the brain is the principal sexual organ."[12]

It is also in the light of this evolutionary principle that one must understand Aristotle's opinion that sexual intercourse is an inferior good because it involves an abdication of reason. Copulation, which in its human beginnings was a brute act,[13] during the Christian era has been artificially controlled by religious and social constraints; but in the present age it is finding its basic order not in any external and institutional requirements but in the demands of the human person as person. This whole evolutionary process has paralleled and been nourished by the emergence of a sense of selfness and of interiority in western man. In that process — what Aristotle called "reason" and what we would call "spirit" has taken possession of itself — the old assumption of sexuality as a rupturing force in a world of continuity, an assumption defended in our time by Max Picard,[14] has been set aside. Discontinuity is a characteristic of matter, of that world of the absolutely "physical" which is essentially fragmentary and which is defined as part-outside-of-part. And so long as sexuality was understood on that plane only, the Aristotelian notion of "abdication of reason" was valid. But with the emergence of spirit, with the conscious awareness of human interiority, the purely genital act has more and more come under the regency of the whole human person. It is in fact the meaning of the present sexual revolution — which has its counterpart in every aspect of human

---

[12] Cited by A. Plé, O. P., in Vie affective et chastété (Paris, 1963), p. 176.

[13] It is noteworthy that Leo XIII, speaking of the corruption of marital love among the pagans, emphasized that "the wife had sunk so low" that she was viewed only "as a means for the gratification of passion, or for the production of offspring" (Arcanum Divinae Sapientiae, 7; italics added).

[14] Hitler in Ourselves (Hinsdale, 1947), pp. 190–191.

activity — that sexuality must transcend its merely biological limitations.

By way of one specific application of these large statements, it may be suggested that what the sexual revolution implies is a kind of space-time continuum with regard to conception and contraception, even as it more obviously implies a continuum of the primary and secondary ends of marriage. In the classic philosophy time and space exist because of matter or its analogues. Yet because of a primitive folk cosmology space has been viewed by Catholics as more "material" than time: a spatial object is obviously palpable and visible — as when we think of the disciples literally seeing Christ "ascend into heaven"; whereas temporal reality is intangible, seemingly ethereal, and therefore more "spiritual." Thus a directly contraceptive practice which places an obstacle in time, such as the "safe period," is moral, while a practice which places an obstacle in space is absolutely forbidden. What is imperative is to recognize the common material root of the temporal and the spatial and their subordinate role in the service of spirit.

Moreover, this entire evolutionary development has even affected canonists and moral theologians, no matter how ingeniously they may attempt to cling to certain historical formulations as absolutes. Thus for many centuries the "natural" use of sexuality meant for the official teachers a use which in no way and in no circumstances interfered with the physiological processes. Once coitus, whether voluntary or involuntary, had been engaged in, any attempt to frustrate the biological order was viewed as immoral. Whereas in the present, under the influence of humane sentiments and quite apart from any subsequent rationalizations, many theologians now teach that a woman who has been raped may make use of a vaginal douche with the direct intention of expelling the alien and unwanted seed. Thus the "natural" use of sexual powers no longer means, as it did for theologians before the twentieth century, their functioning entirely apart from the will and intention of the subjects, entirely, that is, as mechanical acts so that any interference with the "machinery" would be regarded as intrinsically immoral. And there is at least one moralist, Charles McFadden O.S.A., who would extend this concern for the innocent victim of rape to permitting the use of an intrauterine spermicidal douche. The justification for this is:

> . . . ovulation occurs only once a month, that a month involves about 720 hours, and that the ovum possesses a life-span of, perhaps, eighteen hours (some authorities would place it as low as twelve hours, others as high as twenty-four hours), we are confronted with the fact that the odds are about 40 to 1 against a live ovum being present at the time of rape.[15]

Since this author has gone to great lengths to explain that any fertilized egg is in every sense of the word a human person with all the rights of a person, and that therefore destruction of the fetus is simply murder, it is difficult to follow the reasoning that would say that even on the basis of a remote possibility, that is, on the basis of a forty-to-one chance, it would be permissible to use a spermicide which would directly kill a fetus if present. Yet however hesitant one may be about embracing this line of argument, it is only necessary here to point out the radically greater willingness there is now than in the past to interfere with the "natural" ends of the sexual act.

A similar such evolution is evident in Pius XII's condemnation of the practice of homologous insemination whereby the seed drawn directly from the testicles or derived in some other licit manner, is inserted in the genital tract of the wife. The condemnation is not so important here as is the basis for it:

> We formally prohibit artificial insemination in marriage. The conjugal act by its natural structure is a personal relation, an immediate and concurrent collaboration by the husband and wife who as such and in accord with the nature of the act express by it that reciprocal gift which according to the sacred Scriptures engenders "union in one flesh only."[16]

On the ground, then, of the secondary end of marriage, the attainment of the primary end was interdicted by Pius XII. If that is so, it is not entirely impossible that on those same grounds of "union in one flesh only" a similar interdiction of the attainment of the primary end would be allowable in other cases of great necessity. The Pope himself went on to explain that the marriage bond did not confer a right to "artificial impregnation," but only a

---

[15] Medical Ethics (Philadelphia, 1961), p. 144.
[16] Address to the Italian Catholic Union of Midwives, AAS 43, 1951.

right to the "natural marital act"; the slight shift in accent is important because the natural marital act is not being defined as the depositing of the semen in the vagina with the direct intention of procreating, it is now being defined in terms which can only be characterized as highly personalistic.

However, everything depends, again, on the definition of "natural," for the Pope added that the "marriage contract has not the 'child' for its object, but the 'natural acts' which are able to beget new life and are destined for that end." Yet an act using a contraceptive is intrinsically no more able to beget new life than is an act posited during an assuredly "safe period." Moreover, it is impossible to say that a pre-determined safe period is either intrinsically or by the intention of the agents "destined for" procreation. It is, then, to the role of natural law that one must always return; and it is with some reflections on this theme and on its relation to ecumenism that I would like to close this portion of the present discussion.

It is a tenet of the natural-law doctrine as developed by Catholic moralists that the primary principle, "avoid evil and do good," is known by all men whose reason is normally developed. Secondary principles which are direct deductions from the first principle are also regarded as knowable by all men of reason. Concerning the tertiary principles, which are "conclusions of rather involved processes of reasoning,"[17] it is affirmed that a man of developed reason may at times be invincibly ignorant of some of them; this ignorance will, it is alleged, be due to the influence of immoral customs, generally accepted evil practices, etc. There is some circularity to the argument here as well as some dubious sociology, since it is not clear how the initiators of the "immoral customs" and "evil practices" could have disseminated them so broadly and have given them such widespread currency in the face of the developed reason of all other members of society. It is also difficult to see why honest and objective investigators, seeking to set aside so far as possible their prejudices, could not work their way back through the customary evil practices to a determination of the pristine virtues. That in point of fact they have

---

[17] Thomas J. Higgins, S.J., *Man as Man: The Science and Art of Ethics* (Milwaukee, 1948), p. 121.

not suggests that the natural-law doctrine is really a kind of gnosis attainable only by the initiates of the mystery.

Otherwise how explain that contraception is not universally acknowledged as immoral, particularly since the principle on which it is condemned entails no "complicated processes of reasoning"? Rather it involves only the most elementary enthymeme: the essential purpose of the conjugal union is procreation, and therefore any frustration of that purpose is immoral. The crux of the problem is not a matter of accurate or defective reasoning, but of the basic premise. Regrettably, the attainment of such basic premises is not the work of ratiocination, but of revelation, intuition, instinct, or cultural conditioning. To avoid a wholesale condemnation of the great majority of non-Catholics, natural-law theorists would have to say that the evil of contraception falls under the tertiary conclusions of the natural law. But it is apparent that so far as the distinguishing note of tertiary conclusions goes — the complexity of the reasoning involved — it may as well be viewed as falling under those of the secondary order. One Catholic moralist has even stated that:

> . . . a principle of the natural law is: Foster offspring; unite with the opposite sex in a union of love; avoid anything that would be contrary to the natural use of this power of procreation, that would be contrary to the natural attraction existing between male and female. . . .[18]

Of this and similar principles enumerated, this author observes that they "are as self-evident as the most fundamental principle *do good and avoid evil.*" In this instance contraception would be directly included in those acts which are "contrary to this natural power of procreation." Thus if we root the intrinsic immorality of contraception in *any* principles derived from the natural law, whether primary, secondary, or tertiary, we must conclude that no man of normally developed reason can be invincibly ignorant of the unnatural character of this evil — a conclusion which necessarily foredooms any ecumenical efforts on the part of Roman Catholics.

One may also consider the following similar ecumenical barrier that the present natural-law argument raises. Catholic moralists

---

[18] Michael V. Murray, S.J., *Problems in Ethics* (New York, 1960), p. 234.

teach that for a couple to enter into marriage with the intention of bestowing on each other only the right to contraceptive intercourse is to render the marriage invalid. (We have seen only recently in a decision of the Roman Rota how exemplarily this principle can be invoked to ease the strained consciences of multi-married celebrities.) Let us suppose two people refuse to accept the distinction between "natural" sexual relations and contraceptive intercourse — since we know it is perfectly licit to have intercourse without the *intention* of procreating — would their marriage be valid? If this is so on the ground of natural law, then the inference would be applicable to overwhelming numbers of non-Catholics, all of whom must therefore be viewed by *their* separated brethren as living, at least formally, in a state of concubinage.

Since the natural law is the expression of the divine mind, there can be no cancelling of any part of it, for such cancellation would be a contradiction and a denial of the existence of a supreme lawgiver. But Catholic moral philosophers do teach that divorce and polygamy — also seemingly inalterably condemned by natural law — may be allowable in certain circumstances. The Pauline privilege allows what is by strict definition divorce; and polygamy was sanctioned by Moses. In both instances the Catholic natural-law theorist maintains that this does not mean the natural law admits of exceptions, but rather that what unaided reason has attained, in concluding to the immorality of divorce, is erroneous; for, according to these moralists, natural law does not say, do not grant divorces; what it says is, do not grant divorces unless the supreme lawgiver approves. Obviously, such a notion makes the classic notion of natural law absurd, since it either means that only explicit biblical revelation and the Church which interprets it can verify the nature of natural law, or it means that God's mind can change. Both illations are untenable, and the only humanly logical line to follow is that many of the premises employed by natural-law theorists as well as many of the conclusions deduced are false. This is to say quite explicitly that we have not yet discovered entirely what the supreme lawgiver approves: this is hardly surprising, since the rational faculty which is the proper discerner of natural law is itself in a process of self-discovery.

It is not possible to conclude any treatment of natural law and contraception without taking up in some detail the argument proffered by Germain Grisez in his book on the subject.[19] Professor Grisez of Georgetown writes his criticism of contraception from the viewpoint of an "untraditional" natural-law theorist. He goes about his task in a tidily business-like way, first setting forth some of his own credentials:

My wife, Jeannette, and I married thirteen years ago. At that time I was just entering studies for the degree of Doctor of Philosophy. We now have four children, the oldest twelve and the youngest six. Life has not been easy during all of these years. Yet we have survived without contraception, and we think the conviction that we had to survive and could survive without it has been essential to doing so.

Husband and wife, to use some earlier imagery of the book, were not "goaded onto wrong paths by enthusiasms over the greener pastures projected in an illusory light by the latest phantasms of secular thought." Being thus armored in these durable orthodoxies, Professor Grisez adds a kindly admonition for many of his readers, "Those not accustomed to subtle argument, as well as those who do not respect reason, will be little moved by what I have to say. Against the heart reason has little power, and it is just as impotent against sentimentalism which has become confused with charity as it is against plain ill will."

The subtlety of the argument is immediately evident in Professor Grisez's derivation of the fundamental and absolutely basic principles of morality from our knowledge of man's intrinsic inclinations. He inquires: "What are all the inclinations with which man is endowed prior to acculturation or any choice of his own?" He then notes that this "question requires and can be settled only by empirical inquiry."

Fortunately, psychologists, despite their theoretical disagreements, have come to a remarkable consensus that human motivation presupposes a number of basic inclinations.

Although these inclinations are classified and named in different ways by different authors, they tend to form a list which can be summarized as follows. Man's fundamental inclinations are: the tendency to preserve life, especially by food-seeking and by self-defensive behavior; the tendency to mate and to raise his children; the tendency to seek certain experiences which are enjoyed for their own sake; the tendency to develop skills and to exercise them in play

---

[19] *Contraception and the Natural Law* (Milwaukee, 1965).

and the fine arts; the tendency to explore and to question; the tendency to seek out the company of other men and to try to gain their approval; the tendency to try to establish good relationships with unknown higher powers; and the tendency to try to use intelligence in guiding action.

Anthropological investigation only confirms what psychology states. In fact, these basic motives are the topics according to which anthropological investigations commonly are conducted. This is so precisely because these motives are the principles which collectively define whatever human life possibly could be.

By interpretation these basic data give rise to "principles of practical reason" which constitute the unchanging norm of morality. These principles demand only that the "human possibilities they establish should be maintained." This maintenance requires in Professor Grisez's theory that no action can be taken against one basic principle "in order to maximize another." Contraception is evil, therefore, because it maximizes the value of interpersonal communion by acting directly gainst the "good of procreation." Unfortunately it is never made very clear why an isolated contraceptive act placed in the context of a marriage consciously dedicated to the "good of procreation" is itself intrinsically immoral, particularly when such an act may be directly aimed at that good of procreation which derives from the basic inclination to "raise children."

Professor Grisez recognizes some order among these various principles, but it is an order of a highly republican character: all of the principles are in effect created equal. Perhaps a more apt figure than a republican polity would be that of an anarchy in which, though some principles are more equal than others, they all possess the same power of vote and veto. But one may wonder, however, whether a more genuinely human ethical structure would not be better patterned after a constitutional monarchy in which there is a hierarchy of values all subordinated to the ruling principle which is not the Good as such, but the free exercise of the human spirit.

Like most descriptive metaphysicians, Professor Grisez is correct in his affirmations but weak with regard to what he has negated. One feels he has said something, but left unsaid much more. If we are talking about a genuinely "empirical inquiry" into man's basic inclinations we must know, for example, what "men" were studied, what were the sample groups considered, how representative were they, what were the controls employed, how rigorous was the methodology, etc. It is something less than cogent to say that psychologists and anthropologists agree on such or such, and to casually supply as verification references to a couple of textbooks in psychology and anthropology. Moreover, how can one determine what it is with which "man is endowed *prior* to acculturation," if those making the determination are themselves products of an obviously long-term acculturation? And if acculturation is one of man's distinctive attributes, to abstract from it may leave one with a definition of man which is applicable to no living human being. The danger in this kind of shorthand investigation is that one may end up with only an amorphous residue, only an en-bloc brute distillation, only a crude common denominator, more or less acceptable only to the degree that it may mesh with one's own personal "sentimentalism."

One notes, for instance, among these empirical inquirers a rather considerable lacuna: we have psychologists of a certain persuasion — strong on Freud and Adler, weak on Jung — and anthropologists; but no sociologists. This neat discrimination makes the classification of fundamental inclinations more representative of primitive urges, and therefore wondrously well-adapted to bolstering up a primitive — or, in nicer prose, "traditional" — doctrine. And in fact, apart from the last added item — "the tendency to use intelligence in guiding action" — Professor Grisez's list could have been assembled by the careful observation of any anthropoids. Even a little sociology would make one wary of these global reductionist theories; and even a little zoology — perhaps even some belles-lettres: e.g., *After Many A Summer Dies the Swan* — might lead other empiric inquirers to a radically different notion of what man's basic inclinations are. The peril in these approaches to descriptive metaphysics is the philosopher's penchant for ultimately relying on his own educated impressions and selective hunches to peg his predetermined thesis. Since there is no quarrel here with Professor Grisez's belief that basic human inclinations become primary principles of morality by intuitive discernment rather than by theoretical reflection, it is necessary to concentrate on this pivotal question of what are man's "basic human inclinations" — prescinding for present purposes from the larger question (in order that the discussion may be carried on within Professor Grisez's chosen framework) of whether one can adequately define man as anything other than the "undefinable."

The arbitrary character of these "descriptions" is brought out in a statement much later in the book: "There is little use for a proponent of contraception to appeal to psychology at this point. Some psychologists have been influenced by their own ideology with regard to sexual activity and also by various situationist philosophical views." But if some psychologists have, then some haven't: on which ones can we depend in determining *basic* human inclinations, and what pre-basic criterion do we use to justify our dependence? The quoted passage above is followed immediately by this: "More relevant is the almost universal agreement of the sages that the psychic drive for sexual release must be mastered if man is to become fully human." Those not accustomed to subtle argument may hesitate over this juxtaposing of "sages" and "psychologists": is it that "psychologists" have been influenced by their own ideology," while sages suffer no such trammel? Actually the distinction between psychologists and sages is as subtle and just as rhetorically functional as the distinction between logic-choppers and philosophers, gerund-grinders and poets, ward-bosses and public servants. The bias implicit in the very choice of words — "psychologists" v. "sages" — makes it clear that what Professor Grisez is really opposing are, in his unspeakable terms, "modern novelty" and "traditional wisdom": or in my own ineffable coinage, "science" and "folklore."

One gets curious as to exactly which psychologists have contradicted the sages' view that "the psychic drive for sexual release must be mastered if man is to become fully human." Many would have thought the problem to be one of *how* sexual release is to be mastered and what direction that mastery should take. By name who are these psychologists? One fears that we are here once again back among the textbooks, among the *Playboy* scholars and the M-G-M Freuds. But the more relevant conclusion is the commonplace that the "universal agreement" of the sages is a fiction: the agreement of the sages in one age is their disagreement in the next — it could even be that the psychologists of one age may be the sages of the next.

Professor Grisez's polarizing of past and present (sages v. psy-

chologists), and his uneasiness at the apparent opposition of
the two, raise what is the underlying and fundamental issue in
the entire debate over the morality of contraception: the significance of the development of human consciousness. Professor
Grisez pays due homage to the principle of evolution and em-
braces with enthusiasm most of his putative opponents' dynamic
conceptions about "the fact that human nature really is changing."
Yet oddly enough for one who adopts a consistently more-holistic-
than-thou attitude in the face of the dangerous "dualism" of
Canon Janssens, Professor Grisez can declare that "in man we
find an evolution not of organism but of spirit" — an observation
which collides disastrously with an earlier affirmation that "man
is one nature, not two, and his life is not divided between the
conscious life of personality and the material processes of an
organism." The contradiction is more evident in that we have
also been previously told that man is "an organism whose highest
integration is that of rational intelligence." What then is the
meaning of the distinction in the quotation above that "in man
we find an evolution not of organism but of spirit?"

Professor Grisez is quite severe with Canon Janssens and other
"situationists" because of their acceptance of the notion that man
is an "incarnate spirit," and he takes Janssens to task for the
following statement: ". . . because man is an incarnate spirit, even
the bodily aspects of his sexuality have an intrinsic sense diverse
from that of the animals, for these aspects participate in his spiritual interiority . . .": of which Grisez says, "This explanation
implies, of course, the dualistic pre-supposition that apart from
their participation in man's spiritual interiority the bodily aspects
of human sexuality are little better than animal functions." But
if one weighs the two statements it becomes apparent that it is
the Professor and not the Canon who is the dualist, for he seems
to believe that the "bodily aspects of human sexuality" apart
from their relationship to man's interiority can even be a subject
of consideration, can even constitute a reality. It entails a radical
and dangerous dualism merely to toy with the notion that one
could conceive of the "bodily aspects of human sexuality" in
some pure state where they do not participate in man's spirit.
Moreover, if by some miracle of abstraction one could so conceive
of them, it is patent that they would not be better than animal

functions, they would be *inferior* to them, and this precisely because of their deracinated character, because of their essential
incompleteness. One muses over what Professor Grisez's dualism
would do to the agreement of the "sages" on the traditional doctrine of separated substances.

It is this dualism, while allowing some play to the evolutionary
drive — but perhaps, only as an accommodation to ineluctable
fact — which requires that Professor Grisez should discover a
greater "spiritualization" of man only within the ambit fixed by
his predetermined "basic principles." Relapsing into what he has
previously derided as "conventional natural law theory," Professor
Grisez supplies a number of examples to illustrate the ethical
implications of his axiologically harnessed evolutionary factor. Of
these examples the reader is told that they "could be multiplied
endlessly, because the body of derived principles of the moral
law is vast, and this entire body is potentially subject to change."
(One remarks in passing the paradox that this "body" but not
the basic principles admits of change, whereas with regard to man it
is not the "body" but only the basic principle — the human spirit
— which can evolve.) The first two of these examples are generally acceptable, though they may raise problems in moral theology: we are told first "that usury — the taking of interest as
such — *has become* moral because modern man is not the same
as pre-modern man in regard to the realities which are expressed
in modern business and a technologically grounded economy."
Professor Grisez notes, secondly, that "it is true to say that ob-
scurantism in relation to theoretical truth *is becoming* very seriously immoral." Fair enough. It is the third example that evokes
wonder: ". . . it is true to observe that slavery *has become* immoral
because man has changed." (Emphasis added in each quotation.)
But again, unless one subscribes to an absolute dualism, it is
difficult to see how one can affirm that slavery "has become" immoral. It seems incontestable that slavery by definition frustrates
all of those basic principles of morality which, according to Professor Grisez, always remain firm. But this example is even more
devastating for Professor Grisez's larger argument. For if slavery
has become objectively immoral, and therefore at one time *was
not* objectively immoral, it can only be because slaves had *de facto*
as well as *de jure* no human rights; but if they had no human

rights, they could not be defined as human beings. And thus those enslaved primates (which we in our rather clumsy and mistaken modern way might call "people) would have been entirely justified in practicing contraception, particularly since their "motives" — like those of captured animals — would have been of the very highest character, that is, to avoid having offspring born into a state of enslavement. If this is true then there was a time when direct contraception was permissible among the anthropoids to whom, as we have already seen, our original scale of "basic inclinations" was applicable.

We have to do with a peculiarly flexible moral system here: slavery which affronts the whole constellation of man's basic inclinations was once not objectively immoral: but contraception always was and always will be intrinsically immoral since it violates that "good of procreation" which "seems to have been as well understood by the primitives as it is by us." What does this logical and ethical morass tell us about the present natural-law philosophy? It tells us, if nothing more, that it is an admirable instrument for rationalizing many of the worst abuses of Christian moral theology.

Finally, to take the last example of this evolutionary factor as it relates to morality, Professor Grisez observes that "divorce and polygamy once were not seriously wrong because the mutuality in human friendship which Christian man's sexual activity requires apparently was not required by the sexual activity of the pre-Christian man. Our newer humanity makes greater psychological demands, and these indicate the necessity that the sexual relationship between man and wife be perpetual and exclusive." Thus once again does philosophy selflessly come to the rescue of some otherwise embarrassing biblical données. Yet if one can accept such a radical evolution with regard to the licitness of divorce, on the same grounds one ought to be able to argue that those "greater psychological demands" would allow the marital union to be oriented away from, though not against, the good of procreation. But more significantly, at least as far Professor Grisez's own premises are concerned, one may well maintain that divorce was always wrong — even "seriously" wrong: an adverb not applied to the institution of slavery — because, as our conventional natural-law morality has said, divorce violates the child's right to that

freedom which can normally be rightly cultivated only in a monog-
amous union.

We do need a natural-law theory of sexuality. And one may
agree with Professor Grisez that the conventional elaboration of
that theory is seriously defective; but it is not evident that his
own effort carries us much beyond the position of the traditional
manuals. What needs to be articulated is a doctrine which can
mediate between the immobilism of books like the present one
and the relativism of a totally situationist ethic. Fortunately the
direction in which we must travel has already been charted: "The
realization of the requirements of human perfection or of the
content of natural law is a historical *processus*. It is developed
with cultural progress which conditions it, and which in turn it
must orient towards the enrichment of human dignity"[20]

In conclusion it is to be hoped that what the magisterium will
do, given the widespread confusion the present position has
created, is make a simple decree leaving this whole area open to
further exploration, and allowing the determination of specific
means of birth limitation to be left to the judgment of individual
married couples. Psychologically, this would be advisable because
it would be a clear indication that Catholics have finally shucked
off that tutelage which often in the past seemed to require a
manual of casuistry to assess the licitness of a particular act. Sociologically, this would be advisable because it would create a counter-
current to the present clerically imposed orthodoxies, and thus
result in a genuine *consensus fidelium*. Most important of all,
sacramentally such a decree would be advisable because the whole
basis of religion is that union of God with his people which is
figured forth in the marriage bond. The union of the couple is
a sacred sign of the promised return to integrity from the state
of the divided image in which man after the fall has had to live.

For all these reasons one may criticize those laymen who have
seen little benefit in an authoritative statement that would leave
this issue to "private conscience" — worded in those terms, of
course, one may agree. But in fact there is no such thing as "private
conscience." As the French word *conscience* illustrates, conscience
is not just the inner moral imperative, but is the ethical and intel-

---

[20] Louis Janssens, *Liberté de conscience et liberté religieuse* (Paris, 1964),
p. 66.

lectual response of the entire human person to all outside stimuli. Conscience in this sense is not rightly formed by definitive decrees to which the will must demand submission, but by a multiplicity of factors of which authority is only one. To suggest that the magisterium should leave the specifics of birth limitation to the consciences of the couples involved is not to advocate a subjective morality or a situation ethic, for morality is not subjective in any sense; its norms are eternal and unchanging. But our apprehension of them can only be by personal appropriation, and for this no other man or institution can be substituted.

VI

ANTISEMITISM AND
THEOLOGICAL ARROGANCE

When in *Herder Correspondence* for June, 1965, I reviewed Edward Flannery's *The Anguish of the Jews*,[1] several avenues of approach were open for discussing such a book. For example, one might have related it to current politico-moral issues by showing how the methods and styles of antisemitism offer a clear parallel with those of anticommunism and segregationism. Thus when Fr. Flannery observed that under Torquemada "elaborate regulations were set forth for detecting Judaizers. A list of thirty-seven clues was published to help ferret them out. . . . Thirty days of grace were given for self denunciation" (p. 138), one might have remarked, how like the days of McCarthyism. Similarily with Fr. Flannery's summation of the goals of Hitler: "Cleanse the country of Jews and there would be jobs for the unemployed, outlets for professional talent, a new world for youth; industrialists would be more secure in their profits, German maidens would be safe, German nationalism would thrive, and Aryan blood would remain uncontaminated" (p. 210) — one may have noted: how like the days of Governor Wallace or Leander Perez. But a discussion of such parallels, however beneficial it might have been, would not have exposed the actual roots of the problem of Christian antisemitism, and would perhaps even have left the modern Christian, who prides himself on despising McCarthyism and segregation, feeling all the more complacently self-righteous. It was necessary, therefore, to judge Fr. Flannery's book without any Catholic bias in favor of it as an achievement of good wishes and good intentions. On the assumption that there is no judge like

[1] New York, 1965.

a hanging judge, it was necessary to scrutinize the book as closely and assess it as severely as would any conscientious non-Catholic, as would any Jew.

The *Herder Correspondence* review, because it is a necessary prelude to what follows, is included here.

We have to deal with a history of antisemitism by a Catholic priest, and it is this latter element — underlined by the jacket description of the book — which may be presumed to differentiate the present work from other studies of this subject. *The Anguish of the Jews* is conscientiously written, painstakingly researched, and judiciously seeking to avoid extreme judgments; in its overall impact it is an effective critique of antisemitism. Nevertheless it must be said that the book does have the tone, the subtly nuanced flavor, of an *apologia*. Although Fr. Flannery could not even remotely be criticized for having written a *plaidoyer*, a simple exoneration of Christian guilt, nevertheless — and perhaps derivative of his own office as Roman Catholic priest — his impeachment of ecclesiastical authorities is grievously attenuated.

While one never has the impression that Fr. Flannery is intentionally slanting his narrative, the cumulative effect remains that of an enervation of the requisite moral severity. Individual assertions taken separately may be unobjectionable, but the total indictment is vague and diffusive. One does not hear in these pages the accents of Lord Acton's Inaugural Address condemning dilution of moral judgment. Lord Acton defined a standard which, in all charity, one feels *The Anguish of the Jews* cannot quite come up to: "If, in our uncertainty, we must often err, it may be sometimes better to risk excess in rigour than in indulgence, for then at least we do no injury by loss of principle. . . . Opinions alter, manners change, creeds rise and fall, but the moral law is written on the tablets of eternity."[2]

Again, it must be emphasized that in no sense is there any debasing of the moral currency in Fr. Flannery's book; but there *is* an excessive balancing of counterweights that in the end serves to erode firm principles. For example, after a particularly vicious screed of St. Hippolytus to the effect that "because Jews killed the Son of their Benefactor," they will always be slaves, Fr. Flan-

---

[2] *Lectures on Modern History* (London, 1920), p. 27.

nery observes: "No stronger animus than this is displayed in pre-fourth century Christian literature" (p. 38) — as if this were not strong and pernicious enough. Similarly, while deploring the anti-semitic outbursts of St. John Chrysostom, Fr. Flannery also pro-vides an oblique justification by commenting:

The chief venting of his ire was six sermons delivered in his see of Antioch, where *Jews were numerous and influential* and where, *apparently, some* of his flock were frequenting synagogues and Jewish homes and probably trafficking in Jewish amulets. The saint was not one to meet such a situation with equanimity. *Rigid on principle, a born reformer* and a fiery preacher, he threw the whole of his energy and talent into castigating Judaism (p. 47). (*Italics added throughout.*)

Even after the establishment of Christianity as the state religion and when Jews constituted only a very small minority in the empire, Fr. Flannery sees the guilt as equally shared: "Hostilities were brutal and frequent. Blow was met by blow in a scandalous reciprocity of provocation" (p. 56). This exaggeratedly even-handed justice leads the author to remark of this same period: "That some degree of popular hostility toward Jews existed can be concluded from the attacks on synagogues which, as Marcel Simon has pointed out, could not have been instigated by mere ecclesiastical fiat without a response of anti-Jewish feeling in the populace" (p. 58) — as though such popular sentiment were not itself largely the creation of a long sequence of antecedent eccle-siastical fiats. At the conclusion of this section of the book the reader is told: "But in the final accounting the antisemitism of this era, was, *as in the case of pagan antiquity, a reaction* against a vibrant and assertive Judaism" (p. 63). Regrettably few of the texts Fr. Flannery cites will bear out this mitigating judgment. There is a comparably naïve prejudice reflected in the assertion that the relatively benevolent and Christian attitude of Theodoric — denominated, "this *Arian* believer" — must be credited in part to Cassiodorus — denominated, "his *Catholic* and well educated secretary" (p. 70): as though Trinitarian orthodoxy had ever been a guarantee of Christian charity.

Again, we are presented with a complex of suppositious reasons to "explain" an act of horror in the book's treatment of the perse-cution by King Sisebut in Spain: "This monarch, *struggling to*

free his territory from the threat of Byzantine imperialism, probably aware of Jewish 'betrayals' in the East . . . determined to have
done with the Jewish problem once and for all" (p. 73). With
reference to sixth-century France, Fr. Flannery, after remarking
that Jews were "ready on occasion to strike the first blow," finds
it "appropriate" to quote "a thorough student of the period" as
follows: "Even the expulsions and other clearly characteristic
violences inflicted on Jews by representatives of Christianity lose
something of their horror when we discover that Jews, when conditions lent themselves, did not hesitate to have recourse to these
measures themselves" (p. 77). In the light of perennial Christian
claims to a higher morality than that of other religions, this quotation loses something of its "appropriateness."

With an unintended nod to consensus morality, Fr. Flannery
declares of St. Agobard, the author of an incredibly perverse
rant against the Jews: ". . . for some he is an ingrained antisemite,
for others a candid and sincere prelate vindicating the rights of
Christians against an aggressive and favored Jewry leagued with
a philo-Semitic ruler" (p. 83). "Aggressive and favored Jewry"
here describes a group of people seeking only to exercise some very
restricted rights, and "philo-Semitic" describes a monarch intent
on nothing more than treating all his subjects as human beings.
Of this whole period of the dark ages, Fr. Flannery observes:
"The legislation of both Church and state must, in effect, be
seen, above all, [the halting rhetoric betrays the tenuousness of
the conclusion] as a defense against Jewish proselytism" (p. 87).
Moreover, we are told immediately — and irrelevantly — that
"heretics still fared worse than" Jews.

Moving to the beginnings of continent-wide slaughter of Jews
in the late Middle Ages, the opinion is proffered that some of
these massacres "were clearly mob actions, reinforced by religious
fanaticism" (p. 93). One fears that "reinforced" is a euphemism
for "inspired." The bigoted Vincent Ferrer is also euphemisti-
cally characterized as "a miracle worker, an excellent preacher,
and totally dedicated to the conversion of the Jews" (p. 134).
But such "total dedication" led Jews to think of him as a
"scourge": a scourge — Fr. Flannery hastens to remind the reader
— "as much" to the enemies of the Jews as to themselves. This
tissue of palliating circumstances and suppositions is so uncon-

sciously woven by the author and so subtly enmeshes the reader that neither may appreciate the sad irony of the following statement concerning the background of the persecutions in fifteenth-century Poland: "The Church, *naturally*, was alarmed by the ascendancy of the Jews and the preferential treatment they received from the crown" (p. 156). But as in previous instances, this "preferential treatment" consisted merely in the Jews' being "allowed considerable self-government" and in being accepted "as an integral part of Poland. . . ."

Fr. Flannery concludes his book with some general observations on the entire tragedy of antisemitism, and he asserts: "How much more historically plausible it is to see Hitlerian or racist antisemitism as the creature of modern laicism, the modern revolt against God, rather than a fruit of Christian teaching" (p. 275). One regrets that it is necessary to add that such an opinion is "historically plausible" only if one reads history as Fr. Flannery unwittingly but persistently writes it.

To the above remarks I would add two additional quotations from that Catholic historian whom Strachey viciously characterized as an "almost hysterical reviler of priestcraft and persecution"[3] — fortunately we now know that the ethic of Bloomsbury would have led us to the exoneration of an Eichmann. The first quotation is again from Acton's Inaugural Address, and simply reinforces the basis for the preceding indictment we have given of Fr. Flannery's book:

The plea in extenuation of guilt and mitigation of punishment is perpetual. At every step we are met by arguments which go to excuse, to palliate, to confound right and wrong, and reduce the just man to the level of the reprobate. They set up the principle that only a foolish Conservative judges the present with the ideals of the past; that only a foolish Liberal judges the past with the ideas of the present. The mission of that school was to make distant times, and especially the Middle Ages, then most distant of all, intelligible and acceptable to a society issuing from the eighteenth century. There were difficulties in the way; and among others this, that, in the first fervour of the Crusades, the men who took the Cross, after receiving communion, heartily devoted the day to the extermination of Jews. To judge them by a fixed standard, call them sacrilegious fanatics

---

[3] *Eminent Victorians* (New York, 1938), p. 100.

or furious hypocrites, was to yield a gratuitous victory to Voltaire. It became a rule of policy to praise the spirit when you could not defend the deed. So that we have no common code; our moral notions are always fluid; and you must consider the times, the class from which men sprang, the surrounding influences, the masters in their schools, the preachers in their pulpits, the movement they obscurely obeyed, and so on, until responsibility is merged in numbers, and not a culprit is left for execution.[4]

Such, unwittingly — as I have stressed over and over in the above remarks — Fr. Flannery has done. But we must bear in mind also the following from Lord Acton: ". . . scientific thought begins with the separation between the idea and its exponent."[5] For nothing is more apparent than that Fr. Flannery, with the very best of will, with the most noble of intentions, has simply not been able to look upon the Roman Catholic Church's — I emphasize "Church's" — systematic assault on Judaism with the necessary humane detachment and clarity. The reason is that all Roman Catholics, the present writer not excluded, are the products of that unique mindset, cast in the matrix of two millennia of inbred religious paranoia, which can be shattered only by the communal realization that the theology of crusader and conquistador — which, though less noxiously visible, is still our theology — has been a perversion of everything Jesus meant. The shattering of this mindset demands the most deliberate and painstaking therapy aimed at the restoration of an authentic humanism to institutional Catholicism: a humanism, it must be said, which is not sufficiently evident in Vatican II's treatment of non-Christian religions. That twenty centuries of stony sleep "were vexed to nightmare by a rocking cradle"[6] is a truth borne in on all those Christians who shamefully face the fact that the most monstrous crimes in history have been committed either in the name or in the shadow of Jesus of Nazareth.

If there is one lesson that this history teaches it is that the imperialist claims of Roman Catholicism have not brought unity and concord, have not given to men the earthly adumbration of the blessed city of peace. The question must arise in the hearts of Roman Catholics, as it has in the heart of every-

---

[4] Op. cit., p. 24.
[5] Letters of Lord Acton to Mary Gladstone (London, 1913), p. 164.
[6] W. B. Yeats, "The Second Coming."

one that looks from the outside at their Church, whether any historical reality, any temporal organization, can, without succumbing ultimately to collective derangement, harbor in its communal will and in its official declarations the universalist — not *aspirations*, not *pretensions* but — *demands* that Roman Catholicism has asserted. The attrition by pragma, the corruption by contingency, the erosion by passion, that is, the very karma under which humanity labors, makes the mere assertion of such demands in the name of whatever lofty ideology an affront to man's constitution as a being *in history*. Even as pure theory, then, as pure hypothesis, the following from the Declaration on Religious Freedom may be judged faulty — and this, because in history no pure theory or hypothesis exists:

The Church is, by the will of Christ, the teacher of the truth. It is her duty to give utterance to, and authoritatively to teach, that Truth which is Christ Himself, and also to declare and confirm by her authority those principles of the moral order which have their origin in human nature itself. . . . The disciple is bound by a grave obligation toward Christ his Master ever more adequately to understand the truth received from Him, faithfully to proclaim it, and vigorously to defend it. Never — be it understood — having recourse to means that are incompatible with the spirit of the gospel.[7]

It is the very assertion of the claim — be it understood, no matter how gently and benignly enforced — that this historically structured and conditioned body of men can authoritatively teach those principles "which have their origin in human nature itself": it is this very assertion which constitutes a negation of history and of that Incarnation which alone gives history meaning. For if history has one law it is that the full implementing of any absolutist claims necessarily entails "recourse to a means" which is incompatible with them. No contingent means can ever be perfectly compatible with an absolute end.

Enlightened Catholic dogmaticians are perhaps on the way to granting this with regard to Protestantism; and one could imagine some of them arguing in the light of their growing understanding of the temporal that Cardinal Newman would have been right, were he living in the present age, in believing he should have re-

---

[7] No. 14, in *The Documents of Vatican II* (New York, 1966), pp. 694–695.

mained an Anglican because it was in Anglicanism that he found himself, that it was in Anglicanism that Providence and history had placed him. And even with regard to the non-Christian religions, Karl Rahner[8] along with H. R. Schlette[9] has underlined their salvific role; J. R. Geiselmann[10] has emphasized the transmission of revelation through the other great world faiths; and Eugene Hillman[11] has re-established the biblical foundations for envisioning the Church as the sign before the nations and not as the proselytizing agency of conversions. But though the Church is the sign before the nations, it would be very dangerous to say — a danger which the above citation from Vatican II did not successfully skirt — it is the only sign or even the "brightest" sign. To so say would be again to ignore the reality of history, and would ultimately be to succumb once more to the temptation of the Grand Inquisitor and the pogroms that attend inevitably his ministry. For a sign is only a sign to those who find it significant, to those who have eyes to see.

Moreover, the sign which the Church signifies is not a pure sign; it is a sign obscured by its own embodiment. Thus the sign which in fact historical man always is proffered is the sign of an institution, is an institutionalized sign presented to an institutionalized man. One cannot, therefore, say with Père Clérissac that the terms "Church" and "Christ" are simply convertible,[12] any more than one can say that the Church as "the pure sign of Christ" can authoritatively judge what belongs to "human nature itself": neither exists. What does exist is the institutionalized sign and man who has been shaped by his family, his speech, his education, his environment, that is, by all the institutions that play about him and define his history. And this man — there is no other — may find the sign proffered by the Church utterly repugnant. Nor can he be said to be the pathetic victim of "invincible ignorance." That term is meaningless because the truth to which such a man gives himself is the truth to which he has

---

[8] *Theological Investigations* (Baltimore, 1966), V, chapter six.

[9] *Towards a Theology of Religions* (New York, 1966).

[10] *The Meaning of Tradition* (New York, 1966).

[11] *The Church as Mission* (New York, 1966).

[12] *The Mystery of the Church* (New York, 1937), p. 17. It was a comparable theological naïveté which led Père Clérissac to become an ardent advocate of the Action Française before its condemnation.

been conformed by Providence and history, and the falsity which
he rejects, he does so under those same shaping factors. There
exists no other truth or falsity for any man. What Newman said
about certain non-British devotional practices may be applied,
mutatis mutandis, to religious differences: "I venture to say the
majority of Catholics in England know nothing of them. They do
not colour our body."[13]

All of the above may serve to explain why there is something
inherently depressing in such efforts at "Jewish-Christian dialogue"
as are represented, for example, by the recently published Torah
and Gospel[14] and The Star and the Cross:[15] in the end the votaries
of Gospel and Cross, while anxiously and eagerly trying to admire
what Torah and Star stand for, remain enmeshed in their own
exclusivist notions. In fact, in the light of the commission laid
upon them by the Fathers of Vatican II, the Christians in such
encounters must regard themselves as working, however gently,
subtly, obliquely, for the "conversion" of their — not perfidious,
we have been taught to say, but — alas, unbelieving partners. Yet
when one looks at a book such as Conversion to Judaism[16]
— in many ways not a particularly pleasing book, but probably
no more disheartening than scores of Christian handbooks for
"convert making" — and reads testimonials of separation from
Christianity and Catholicism and acceptance of Judaism, one is
not struck by any evidence of ill-will or ignorance. One glimpses
only a faith being achieved, as it can only be, through the medium
of an institution — even as in the case of conversions to Catholicism. What either faith leads to no man has ever been able to
say with certainty. One can only say that it is not faith in an institution but through it.

Nor can the Christian, with a wink of understanding complicity
at his corelegionists, simply declare that here God is writing
straight with crooked lines. In the world as we know it, all lines
are crooked: and all are converging on one point. This is not to
opt for some "higher religion," some syncretist spiritualism à la

---

[13] In Ward, The Life of John Henry Cardinal Newman (London, 1912),
II, p. 180.
[14] New York, 1966.
[15] Milwaukee, 1966.
[16] New York, 1965.

Friedrich Heiler, because the final convergence will not occur in history. On the contrary, what this is saying is that in concrete reality there is no perfect embodiment of truth; every sign, even as it reveals, obscures. And man himself, a chiaroscuro entity, is obliged to give himself only to that truth with which he feels "at home," to that truth to which he has been conformed.

That is why, with regard now only to the Christian churches, one looks at the ecumenical movement with satisfaction and concern; satisfaction that so many prejudices are being uprooted, and concern that — as with a possible world state — there may be no new frontiers, no institutional embodiments for the Christian dissenter, no, as they used to be called, "free churches." In such a christendom both because of its amalgamated power and because the creative tension between polar viewpoints will have been dissolved, the non-Christian will have all the more to fear. "It is not good to forget over what gulfs the spirit/Of the beauty of humanity, the petal of a lost flower blown seaward by the night wind, floats to its quietness."[17] Which is only to say that since it has been in a "world come of age" and in the dawn of the "noosphere" that the greatest mass murders in history have occurred, it is not good to forget how tenuously does institutionalized man hold on to his sanity and rein in his universalist pretensions. It was those pretensions that Christ spurned when he refused to adore Satan, though all the kingdoms of the earth would have been given to him.

I conclude with one further, and more explicitly Roman Catholic, comment on *The Anguish of the Jews*. Early in his book Fr. Flannery notes that the popular cultus of a saint does not necessarily imply that what the saint represented was officially sanctioned by the Church. Thus the attribution of the title "Saint" or "Blessed" to the alleged victims of medieval ritual murders does not imply that the Church has substantiated "the validity of the murder accusation or the historicity of the murders" (p. 100). What it does imply has been brought out in the preceding comments and need not detain us again here. However, the canonization of virulent antisemites does raise a theological problem. For example, John Capistrano was responsible for fomenting murderous riots against the Jews, and he presided at a trial of

---

[17] Robinson Jeffers, "Apology for Bad Dreams."

Jews accused of desecrating a host, during which he personally supervised "the torture of some of the accused from whom confessions to this and other ritual crimes were accepted. In all, forty were burned, a rabbi hanged himself, children of the deceased were taken for baptism, and the remainder were banished" (p. 115). John Capistrano was named among the saints not by popular acclamation, but by formal decree, a decree which dogmaticians maintain is one of the ordinary exercises of the charism of papal infallibility.

Cardinal Newman, engaged throughout his life in the diaconate of the real, the concrete, the historical, feared the proclamation of the pope's infallibility because it gave so much power to one man.[18] How much more fearsome is that power when it is seen as invested in many men, invested in an institution?

---

[18] Cf. Ward, op. cit., II, p. 380.

VII

MARXISM AS PROPAEDEUTIC

It is more and more evident that any rapprochement of Marxists and Christians in the United States will have to begin on the level of ideas rather than of action. If the editors of so presumably a liberal journal as *The New Republic*, in an otherwise balanced treatment of various public demonstrations against the war in Vietnam, could go off on a gratuitous excursion chiding the Students for a Democratic Society for their indifference to Communist infiltration,[1] it is obvious that even on the enlightened left there can be no common front with Marxists in any cause no matter how laudable and no matter how pure the Marxist contribution may be. Nor is this in any way surprising. The wounds of the past have not yet healed; and it cannot be denied that many of the tactics and goals of American Marxists in the past offer not the slightest foundation for mutual trust in the future.

Yet there are dangers in living in the past and in assuming that while oneself is progressing in wisdom one's enemies remain always the same — John XXIII ought to have proved a better instructor in history than this. Though the old anticommunist

---

[1] "We shall be seeing a variety of demonstrations and counter-demonstrations in coming weeks. Respecting their constitutional rights to assemble, speak and petition does not mean respecting every tactic that is used. In our judgment, for example, the Students for a Democratic Society do themselves and their aims a disservice by welcoming Communists in their ranks, and by making a virtue out of indifference to the possibility of Communists becoming the dominant voice in their organization. The experience of the liberal and labor movements with Communist infiltration in the '40's ought not to be brushed aside as irrelevant. And although the Sino-Soviet split has spawned varieties of Marxists today, and the term 'Communist' is far more ambiguous than it was during the Korean war, a clear distinction remains between the advocates of a democratic society and those who wish to destroy it." *The New Republic* (October 30, 1965).

slogans continue to be invoked with all the vigor of a decade-
and-a-half ago, and the communist menace continues to provide
a livelihood for its professional exorcists, most Americans would
be hard put to define exactly what in the immediate present is
the nature of this continuing conspiracy and in what specifically
its present danger lies. Nevertheless, and understandably, given
the tardy irreversibility of any obsolete popular assumption,
there is little possibility of even the most innocuous active collaboration between American Marxists and any significant group
within American society.

But how, then, is conversion to be wrought? How is any kind
of modification, any kind of development or regression to be
achieved? We can hardly expect presumably desirable ameliora-
tions to result from the unending treatment of Marxists as in
effect criminally and incurably insane. We cannot anticipate any
improvement if the only curative offered by those who boast
of the soundness of their own health is incarceration or isolation.

If there cannot be collaboration, there must at least be collision
of antagonist views, there must at least be encounter on the
level of ideology and of idea.[2] For the elementary truth is that
conversation is not contamination; and since talk is cheap even
the most fundamentalist Birchers should not begrudge their
Christian neighbors some slight expenditure. But a difficulty considerably more grave than the widespread opposition to any
discussion with communists whatever is raised by the fact that
every dialogue assumes at least a minimum of shared beliefs,
and it does seem that between a professed atheist and a professed
theist all common ground has been eroded. Disregarding for a
moment the haziness attached to any definition of "atheism"
— for it is patent that an atheist totally committed to the *en
avant* is by the fact committed to the *en haut*[3] — and assuming

---

[2] For the radical need of dialogue on the social plane, see Louis Janssens,
Liberté de conscience et liberté religieuse (Paris, 1964), pp. 120 ff; for a
phenomenology of dialogue between believer and unbeliever, see Maurice
Bellet. *Ceux qui perdent la foi* (Paris, 1965), part one.

[3] Of the Christian "en haut" and the Marxist "en avant," Teilhard remarks: "Two religious forces from now on colliding in the heart of every
man; two forces, we have just seen, which are weakened and dissipated if one
isolates them." "Le coeur du problème," in *L'Avenir de l'homme* (Paris,
1959), p. 345.

for the moment that the "religious" barrier *is* insuperable, one may still wonder why men in controversy must seek to locate their community of interests in a factor which, no matter how primary some may feel it to be in reality, is secondary in their own experience: why, that is, Christian and Marxists must seek a common ground in their diverging approach to the notion of a supreme being. The theological idea of God is so cluttered with ecclesiastical and sociological accretions, and the idea of Marxist atheism is so encumbered with the animus of eighteenth and nineteenth century conflicts, that in the present both ideas are largely cultural constructs — which, like all constructs, ought to be periodically razed.

The common basis for any discussion of essentials must be a datum which is, so far as possible, unmediated by anything ideological or notional. This datum is the human experience of itself. What is radical to Marxist and Christian is not their rejection or acceptance of the idea of God as such, but rather their sense of man in history. When Teilhard said that what is of importance in Marxism is not its atheism but its humanism, he implied also that what is of importance in Christianity is not its "theism" but its humanism;[4] for it is only through humanity and its achievements that a Christian can affirm his belief — not in theism but — in a divine person. For the Christian as for the Marxist it is in history that man comes to know himself and all else. And it is in the analysis of this common commitment to the making of history, to the work of the temporal that Marxist and Christian meet.

Such an analysis will bring out that for neither the Marxist nor the Christian can this work be conceived of as something undertaken for "social betterment," as a kind of patronizing surveillance and domination of the earth; to so conceive it would be to fall victim to the colonialism of the intellect. It is not, then, a work done merely to assure a sharing in the "fruits of

---

[4] Cf. "Consider at this moment the two extremes: here a Marxist and there a Christian, both convinced of their particular doctrine, but both also, one presumes, radically motivated by an equal faith in man. Is it not certain, is it not a fact of everyday experience, that these two men, precisely to the degree that they believe (that they feel each other to believe) strongly in the future of the world, experience one for the other, man to man, a fundamental sympathy?" "La Foi en l'homme," *Ibid.*, p. 242.

the earth," though this is its necessary concomitant. Nor therefore can it be a work done *in order to* bring about either a socialist utopia or the New Jerusalem; it is not ordained immediately to some programmatic future, whether that future be defined as the classless society or the Omega point. This work is undertaken for no ultimate temporal achievement, though temporal achievements are its surest signs, but simply because it is, unselfconsciously, unprogrammatically in the very act of "spiritualizing" reality — others may prefer to say "ordering," "organizing," "transforming" — that man exercises best his own humanity and so grows up to his full stature;[5] and so approximates, the Christian would say, the ideal man: Christ.

It is in the implications of their engaging in the work of the world that Christian and Marxist can find a common basis for dialogue. "The mystical body of Christ," Pius XII wrote, "as the members who constitute it, does not muffle itself in the abstract, outside the fluctuations of space and time; it is not and cannot be separated from the world which surrounds it."[6] And this, because it is *in* the world that the mystical body achieves self-understanding. Tawney has, not without some derision, observed that, "The last of the Schoolmen was Karl Marx."[7] The *mot* is justified because it was St. Thomas who emphasized that, "It was a serious error in those of whom Augustine speaks to assume that it does not matter what men think of the created universe so long as they think rightly concerning

---

[5] "What passes from each of us into the mass of humanity by means of invention, education and diffusion of all sorts is admittedly of vital importance. I have sufficiently tried to stress its phyletic value and no one can accuse me of belittling it. But, with that accepted, I am bound to admit that, in these contributions to the collectivity, far from transmitting the most precious, we are bequeathing, at the utmost, only the shadow of ourselves. Our works? But even in the interest of life in general, what is the work of human works if not to establish in and by means of each one of us, an absolutely original centre in which the universe reflects itself in a unique and inimitable way? And those centres are our very selves and personalities. The very centre of our consciousness, deeper than all its radii; that is the essence which Omega, if it is to be truly Omega, must reclaim. And this essence is obviously not something of which we can dispossess ourselves for the benefit of others as we might give away a coat or pass on a torch. For we are the very flame of that torch." *The Phenomenon of Man* (New York, 1959), p. 261.

[6] Text in *Études* (June, 1949).

[7] *Religion and the Rise of Capitalism* (New York, 1947), p. 39.

God. For error in the matter of the universe means false opinion about God. . . ."[8] And while the dimension of history seems seriously lacking in St. Thomas — though less seriously, as Father Max Seckler has shown,[9] than modern critics of Thomism triumphantly proclaim — there is no doubt that his sense of the real causality of creatures and of man as an incarnate spirit represents a more organic view of the worth of the temporal than the oversimplified platonism which preceded and followed him, and which has been enshrined in Christian devotionalism up to the present.

Undoubtedly this shared commonwealth of Marxist and Christian still leaves vast differences that separate the two; but they are largely differences that relate to the indiscernible — though not therefore necessarily unknown — future. What is important is that both Christian and Marxist begin from a compatible notion of man's relation to the world, that both see a kind of salvation through the universe. And just as Christians are now learning that the natural law is not a body of ready-made tenets given from somewhere on high, but a law to be discovered in the concrete events of an evolving history, so the Marxist will learn that the God the Christian worships is not in some "great beyond," but is met in the present actuality of things.

In classical Marxist thought the idea of God, like that of private property, was seen as a force for alienation. But such an idea of God is founded on a distorted theology. The only reality that can alienate man from his true selfness is falsity to what *is*. Man can rebel against some anthropomorphic Jehovah, even against the God of the churches. Man cannot rebel against the being that he is; and if this being that he is, is *somehow* also the being of God, then rebellion against this latter is the only real alienation of self: *Deus est virtualiter ego ipse.* History is written around the attempt to make a doctrine of such rebellion, to set the being of man against the being of God; but no matter how formulated, such an attempt is an impossibility. Regrettably most men think they are living and dying for the formulations, and it is on the level of such formulations that the alleged essential contradiction of Marxism by Christianity is situated.

---

[8] *Summa contra gentiles,* II, 3.

[9] *Das Heil in der Geschichte* (Munich, 1964).

The atheism of the Marxist is only a pseudo-problem for the Christian. Though the Marxist may be convinced that the idea of God alienates man from himself, though he may think the Christian axiom, *homo magis Dei quam sui ipsius,* is only a deceptive tautology — this matters very little: the Christian *knows* better. It will not, of course, convert the Marxist for the Christian to say, as he may and should say, with Cardinal Newman, "I know because I know because I know because I know, etc."; but precisely because the Christian can say this, precisely because he *does* know, he is enabled to recognize this conflict of theism v. atheism as not of the first order, and as certainly no barrier to dialogue. The "drama of atheist humanism" is a drama in the exact sense of not being a reality in life: it is the creation of ideology, scheme, program — again, factors of significance, but simply not of the first significance.

Moreover, to the degree that Marxism is faithful to its humanistic heritage — and no one doubts that its infidelities have been as outrageous as have those of the churches to their own heritage — it is bound to engender a religious attitude among its followers, as Juarès foresaw when he predicted that the fulfillment of the communist ideal would be paralleled by a great religious revival.[10] Religion is defined as a relationship to the sacred, and the "sacred" for Christian and for Marxist can only be defined as the breakthrough of the inferior reality by the superior: the breakthrough of matter by spirit, the Christian would say. The very fact that Marxists believe in a dialectic opens the way to the acknowledgment of "spirit," as is fairly evident from the tortuous logic that has been marshalled, as well as from the tyranny of orthodoxy that has had to be imposed upon Soviet theoreticians, in order to maintain that the dialectic is totally one of matter. But there can be no dialectic without a genuine duality, and thus "diamat" is a contradiction in terms: a conclusion which Gustav Wetter has shown even Marxists are hesitantly beginning to accept — though Fr. Wetter may be faulted for taking philosophical credenda more seriously than they deserve in his gloss on *Divini redemptoris'* condemnation of communism as "intrinsically evil."[11]

---

[10] Cited by Léopold Sédar Senghor, p. 52; see note 12 below.

[11] *Dialectical Materialism* (New York, 1958), pp. 349 ff, and p. 560.

In seeking to affirm the autonomy of man, Marxists have simply been affirming what the Christian would call the transcendence of the human spirit. Religion as well as any other doctrine or program becomes an opiate when this transcendence is frustrated. The religion against which Marxism was originally rebelling was a religion in which in the name of a more or less accurate definition of "God" men turned away from the world, turned away from that act of *spiritualizing* matter — other terms may be supplied ad libitum — in which alone man experiences his being, experiences its contingency and its vocation to the absolute.

It is true the Christian believes he knows this absolute more fully than can the non-Christian; he knows it not merely by the lived experience of his aptitude for it, but also by reason of his belief that this absolute has entered into the contingent in the person of a human being: Christ. The Christian, therefore, believes that there is a terminal point to man's temporal task of spiritualization. But such a belief in no way prevents him from recognizing the immense contribution of those who, while uncertain of the future, have focussed the attention of the world on the work of the world, and who have taught to many Christians the true meaning of ransoming the time. Such a belief not only does not prevent the Christian from seeking a rapprochement with Marxism, it positively invites him to do so.

It is good news, then, that *The Phenomenon of Man* is shortly to appear in a Russian translation. For if it is true that Marxism has taught many Christians the meaning of temporal engagement, and has thus been for them a kind of instructor in salvation-history, it may be equally true that Teilhard will be able to lesson Marxists in the meaning of the eschaton. Such would seem to have been the experience of at least one major Marxist who is now a convinced Teilhardian.

In *Pierre Teilhard de Chardin et la politique africaine*, Léopold Sédar Senghor,[12] President of the republic of Senegal, describes the failure of black racism to provide a constructive alternative to colonialism, and he remarks that Marxism proved to be the first instrument of liberation — though an instrument destined to be superseded: "The essential merit of Marx is not that of

---

[12] Paris, 1962.

having taught us political economy, as one might suppose, but humanism. . . . " Yet "humanism" is an intellectual and an intellectual's ideal, and the broad appeal of Marx to the African Negro was nevertheless economic, it was the provision of a program for breaking with horrors of the kind sketched in *Heart of Darkness* and still existent in Angola and Katanga. The history of the African's disenchantment with Marxism is of little immediate interest here: on the practical level it had to do with the universalist pretensions of communism and its disdain for the notion of negritude, and on a more abstract plane with its affront to the spiritual dispositions of the Africans: "The core of the debate is in the Marxian conception of matter."[13] According to Senghor, Marx's genius lay in realizing the significance of dialectic in history, and, "if Marx had remained in this dialectical vision of the world, if he had gone up to the end of the historical movement, no doubt he would have satisfied our hopes. . . . But he didn't, because his conception of matter remained weighted down by mechanism and his dialectic by logical determinism." Marx's belief that the "world of ideas" is only the material world transposed and translated into the human mind was alien to the African view of reality. Senghor, who is also a distinguished poet, found it repugnant that for Marx "ideas, religion, morality, art are only the 'reflections,' the 'echoes' of material realities, more precisely of economic realities."[14]

It was Teilhard who opened the way out of the dead-ends of classical Marxism as the Africans encountered it. It was Teilhard, Senghor maintains, who showed the Africans the possibility of contributing to the coming universal civilization of mankind without having to sacrifice the values of their "negritude." Nevertheless, the President of Senegal observes, "Teilhard completes Marx more than he contradicts him: he accomplishes Marx's neo-humanism."[15]

The witness of Léopold Sédar Senghor is not unquestionably conclusive mainly because he speaks as one reared in an intellectual tradition which is as much European as it is African but his is an important voice, particularly among those former

---

[13] *Ibid.*, p. 23.   [14] *Ibid.*, pp. 27, 28, 29.
[15] *Ibid.*, p. 34.

colonial peoples who have already sought to develop a native form of socialism. If one believes in scrutinizing the signs of the times for their Christian import, one may find another indication of the role of Marxism as propaedeutic to Christianity in this widespread appeal of communism in precisely those lands where the Christian faith has never been planted. It is a paradox that Marxism has been embraced not in that Western Europe from which it derived its diagnosis of social ills and for which it prescribed its nostrums, but rather in that world which has never known Christianity.

Christian man, like Marxist man, is Antaean man: he must keep in contact with the earth. And even though the Christian believes that Antaeus has a conqueror, that the exclusively Antaean vision must be surpassed in a greater vision, this need not prevent the two giants yoking their forces in the present moment of history. It matters very little *now* that the Christian is convinced of the final impossibility of building here the lasting city and that he must look for another which is to come. It matters very little now that the Christian believes the time will come when the earth shall no longer sustain Antaean man, when he must be lifted up by him who said that if he be lifted up he would draw all things unto himself. Antaeus will be lifted up by that incarnate Word which the Christian poet, Milton, explicitly compared to Hercules.[16]

The Marxist does not believe this and need not believe it now. While eschatology will remain the underlying point of division, it is, by definition, a point which has not yet been realized, a point rooted in the future. In the meanwhile, in the pasch where man presently is, the Marxist can reply to the Christian "expectation of the coming" in the words of Roger Garaudy. "Our task as communists is to crown the highest dreams and the improbable hopes of man; it is to offer them their concrete fulfillment, so that even Christians may find on our earth the beginnings of their heaven."[17]

---

16 "On the Morning of Christ's Nativity," 228.
17 *Cahiers du Communisme* (Juillet- Août, 1963).

VIII

IN DEFENSE OF THE
CATHOLIC UNIVERSITY

Matthew Arnold, anointed Oxonian and professional defender of
"Classics," once venially blasphemed the rival academic loyalties
of Cambridge by remarking: "In the very Senate House and
heart of our English Cambridge I once ventured, though not
without an apology for my profaneness, to hazard the opinion
that for the majority of mankind a little mathematics, even,
goes a long way."[1] It is not so much important to adjudicate this
phase of the Coleridgian-Benthamite conflict, which probably
stretches all the way from Hermes and Apollo to Leavis and
Snow, as it is to draw attention to what would seem a rudimentary datum — were it not so often called into question recently — that universities, as Arnold was obliquely acknowledging,
are constituted by traditions; that is, that they are composed
of votaries of this or that secular and/or religious faith.

Given the current flurry of assaults on the very existence of
the Catholic university, it is therefore desirable that its rationale,
which differs from that of no other university, be sketched almost
geometrically.

Men of like spirit gravitate toward one another and form
communities within the larger society. When these men are
committed to the life of the mind, the common ground they
share becomes the basis for a collegium, for a *universitas magistrorum*; and this is the primary force behind the establishment
of any university, whether it be at medieval Bologna or at present-
day Dallas. The gathering of masters together and the dynamic
diffusiveness of the truths which they have mastered attracts

---

[1] *Culture and Anarchy*, Preface.

disciples, that is, students of the intellectual disciplines; and the result is the *universitas magistrorum et scholarium*. It is from the interaction of these two groups that emerges the ideal *universitas scientiarum*.

It is well to recall these historical commonplaces in the face of present attacks on the very idea of the Catholic university — attacks which have emanated, paradoxically, almost entirely from administrators of Catholic schools. The analyzable content of such attacks has generally been slight;[2] their mode has been a characteristically post-aggiornamento merger of crypto-ecumenism and naïve pluralism; and their upshot — to quote *Newsweek* quoting Norbert Hruby, Vice-President of Mundelein College — has been that, "The less Catholic it is, the better the Catholic college will be":[3] an épatant sentiment which is echoed by Jacqueline Grennan, President of Webster College, in her stylishly attractive advocacy of the elimination of Catholic textbooks from Catholic colleges.

Whatever rhetorical justification these obsolete reactions to a moribund ghettoism may once have had, their strident enunciation now as principles of the new freedom, the new secularism, the new openness, etc., can only serve to obscure the basic rationale for the Catholic university outlined above. Now, again almost geometrically, can be sketched what that rationale is *not*. It is not that a given school is mandated by the ecclesiastical authorities; Fribourg, for instance, though clearly a Catholic university in the deepest sense, is just as clearly not such because it is episcopally sanctioned. In fact, it is rightly designated a "state university" whose Catholic character has nothing to do with ecclesiastical support. That rationale is not that a particular institution is directed by Roman Catholic clergymen; the University of Windsor did not become a Catholic university because it was headed by a Basilian priest. That rationale is not that Roman Catholic theology is taught in a given school, since quite obviously that condition is met by such universities as Yale, Harvard, Iowa, and Wisconsin. That rationale is not that

---

[2] Cf. my discussion in *Continuum* (Spring, 1964) of the keynote address at the annual convention of the NCEA by Paul Reinert, S.J., on "too many Catholic colleges."

[3] June 27, 1965.

Roman Catholic theology is the only theology which is taught, for if that were so, then the Opus Dei University of Navarre could be adjudged a Catholic university — a judgment which would fly in the face of the fact that Opus Dei is a secret society, and therefore by definition subversive of the university ideal. Lastly, and most simply, that rationale is not that a particular school is denominated a "Catholic university" either by itself or by the public; for if that were so, St. John's in Brooklyn would be a Catholic university: a farcical claim in the light of the regression to moral and intellectual barbarism publicly fostered by the officials of that institution.

The fundamental rationale of the Catholic university is the same as that of any other university: that it be not just an aggregation or assemblage of teachers and students, but a true *universitas* magistrorum et scholarium, that is, a body which is organically unified by a common intellectual perspective. One cannot conceive of a university without this unifying principle, because the single mission of the university is to work toward the creation of some kind of synthesis among the various fields of knowledge; this is to say, that it is only the *universitas* magistrorum et scholarium (the unifying intellectual outlook or viewpoint), that can give rise to the *universitas* scientiarum (the synthesis of learning). The intellectual unity of teachers and scholars is the means; the unifying of knowledge is the goal.

Universitas scientiarum does not now mean — any more than it meant to Arnold's Oxford and the Cambridge he was deriding or to Newman's projected Irish university and the University of London against which he was inveighing in the Dublin discourses — that every shade of opinion must be accepted and that every point of view must be inculcated; rather it means that the whole gamut of learning, the encyclopaedeia, be represented within a collegium which is animated by a sufficiently common and unified intellectual vision to draw the disparate disciplines into a oneness. I labor the point: a university is not simply, as Rosemary Lauer seems to think, a place where all subjects are explored; it is a place where all subjects are explored in the light of a single — however broadly conceived — "*principle*": a word which is here used synonymously with "viewpoint," "perspective," "ambiance," "intellectual attitude," etc.

Yet it is this common principle, this very Catholicity of the Catholic university, which has been called into question by recent critics. One can only assume that it is the sub-intellectual activism of administrators, busy currying the foundation heads and quarterbacking among the donors, that can allow them in the name of whatever voguish concept of intellectual freedom and social pluralism to deny to the Catholic university what has never been denied to any university, what is in fact the very essence of the university. For not only is this common perspective the one means of striving after a synthesis among the disciplines, it is also the one means whereby the highest intellectual dialogue can take place: a dialogue not among individuals in a specific academic field, however important, but dialogue between distinct intellectual communities, each of which glimpses the encyclopaedeia by its distinctive light, and each of which can bring this entire gamut of learning *as a whole* into confrontation with that of the other partner. It is therefore for no other reason than that we do live in a pluralist society that we have need of the Catholic university.

It should be added that while it is true such terms as "ambiance," "perspective," "horizon," "viewpoint," have attached to them overtones of vagueness and imprecision, nevertheless this is not weasel currency coined desperately to justify the Catholic university on the loosest and most ambiguous of bases. Rather, those are the only kinds of terms adequate to define what one means by spiritual commitment. Let it be said, then, in agreement with the Grennans and Hrubys that of course there is no such thing as Catholic biology or Catholic economics; but it must be said also that neither is there any such things as the "pure," utterly "objective" biologist or economist. Only the grossest materialism — and *this* is only in style, and manifold in expression, among the administrators of Catholic schools — could sustain the thesis that any discipline, however "empiric," is not colored somehow by the views and attitudes of its practitioners, by their predispositions and "pre-professional" outlooks, that is, by their deepest, most intimately personal understanding of the self in relation to the non-self; in sum, by their "religion."

What that "religion" is for the Catholic university has been the subject of another book by the present writer, and so here it will be necessary only to summarily repeat what is set forth in detail in *The Catholic Dimension in Higher Education*. Such a university has as mission, first, as Newman testified, to supplement and to rectify other sciences by truths of the theological order; second, as Scheeben has pointed out, "inasmuch as faith is concerned with rational truths . . . to guide reason in its domain, by showing it in what direction it must seek the truth."[4] (Which is only to say, as Gilson did of Augustinianism, that Catholics ought not "systematically to blind reason by closing their eyes to what faith shows.")[5] Third, to explore all reality in conformity with the spirit of Christ, who as man acquired knowledge. Fourth, to enter into all salutary areas of human learning to draw them under the headship of Christ — and this, not by way of venal proselytism, but simply of the transfiguration of matter, in the very act of knowing, by the redeemed spirit. It is this organically interrelated structure of ideals and attitudes, along with the truths of revelation, which it is the unique duty of the Catholic university to cultivate. All of this has been said by Dietrich von Hildebrand — in an essay that ought to be required reading in partial fulfillment of the requirements for being a Catholic college president — in so incisive a fashion that it bears being quoted here at length:

The Catholic may never artificially divest himself, even in the use of his natural reason, of the attitude which the *Lumen supranaturale* imparts to him; on the contrary, for the sake precisely of really unprejudiced, objective knowledge and genuinely scientific work, the Catholic cannot follow too much the guiding influence of Revelation in the formation of his fundamental attitude, cannot be too Catholic. Catholic universities are therefore necessary for the sake of truly adequate objective knowledge, not by any means merely for the protection of the religious convictions of the students. They are needed as the institutions where Catholic thinkers and men of science, supported by a truly Catholic environment, informed in their attitude by the spirit of Christ and of His Church, shall be enabled by a really unbiased, truly liberated and enlightened intelligence to penetrate adequately to reality and to achieve by organized teamwork that *universitas* which is nowadays so urgently needed.[6]

It is no argument against any of the above that Catholic

---

[4] *Op. cit.*, section 52, p. 430.

[5] *Introduction à l'étude de Saint Augustin* (Paris, 1929), p. 301.

[6] *The New Tower of Babel* (New York, 1953), pp. 156–157.

universities have more often than not been dedicated to a Catholicism on the most debased level, that they have viewed their mission as the preservation of the ghetto, that they have subverted autonomous intellectual disciplines to one or another arbitrary apologetic posture, that they have acted as the permanent regents of a people forever in a state of tutelage — on the basis of none of this can one accept as fact the now much-repeated bit of shavian punditry which opined that "a Catholic university is a contradiction in terms." In the age of *Pascendi*, as Wilfrid Ward was the first to point out, such a statement may have been true. But abstracting from any particular set of historical conditions, as we simply must if we are to determine the rationale of anything *whatever*, it must be affirmed — and never more vigorously than today — that the term "Catholic university," far from being a paradox, is simply a tautology: the universality and unity of the university are enriched precisely by their being informed by that particular worldview which we call Catholic.

Again, the point bears laboring: this does not mean ecclesiastical supervision, nor the hegemony of theologians or of religious orders, but simply the bond of a common "religion." The whole point of Newman's *Idea* is blunted if it is forgotten that theology, with all it implies, needs the other disciplines as much as they need theology. It is therefore a genuine reciprocity (read: *universitas*) that must exist if the two pitfalls of a bland relativism and a narrow clericalism are to be avoided.

It is in reacting against the latter that we are in danger of embracing the former. That is why one looks with as much suspicion on the current talk about replacing the religious orders with lay boards in the direction of universities as one does on that whole project of de-Catholicizing the schools which was considered above. The religious communities have been guilty of great lapses in the conduct of Catholic universities — with regard to the Vincentians of St. John's hopefully the courts will decide whether there has been guilt of a criminal nature as well. Nevertheless it is not clear that faced by the same circumstances lay groups would have comported themselves with any greater rectitude.

That at least the major religious orders have a unique contribution to make to Catholic higher learning appears self-evident;

for documentation one might read Newman on the Benedictine schools, and for present-day evidence one might look at the record of the Basilians. One is therefore not impressed by Miss Grennan's widely publicized conversion of her college to a lay institution, nor by such quotations as the following from two other college presidents: "Legal control by boards with a majority of lay trustees is definitely the pattern for the future"; "Catholic schools have become public trusts that should reflect the interests, needs and desires of a much broader spectrum of people."[7] If these are just the usual fund-raising proclamations of Catholic administrators who are obsessed with competing with non-Catholic institutions on the one level where competition is foredoomed — endowment and physical plant — then such statements may be dismissed as negligibly opportunistic. But if these are meant to be expressions of serious academic policy, one must inquire what is ultimately to keep the Hiltons, the O'Shaughnessys, the Busches — for who else would predominate on the lay boards? — from exercising the same kind of self-serving institutional power for which the religious communities are now being condemned en bloc. What kind of naïve philo-laicism is it that motivates so many post-aggiornamento clergy and religious to assume that the ordinary human foible is endemic only to their state of life? It was "laymen," these clergy and religious might remember, who were responsible for such abuses of academic freedom as in recent years nearly destroyed the Universities of California and North Carolina. As Newman once said, "A great university ought not to be bullied even by a great Duke of Wellington"[8] — to which one can add, nor even by a great board of lay trustees.

The truth is that administrators think only in administrative categories and therefore cannot see any other solution to the present crisis in Catholic higher education than to shift the authority to a level where they, the administrators, will still retain the accoutrements of office. Whereas what is obviously demanded is that administration be reduced to the performance of its proper housekeeping functions — to maintaining the grounds neat and the buildings clean — and that the actual control of

---

[7] *Newsweek, loc. cit.*

[8] *Apologia pro vita sua* (London, 1902), pp. 14–15.

the institutions be vested in the faculty and its chosen representatives. In too many ways our universities still live in a counter-reformation world, the military world symbolized by St. Ignatius — which is not intended to disparage the Jesuits who, quite simply, constitute the intellect of the American Church. What we have to return to is the ideal of the medieval university, to a world symbolized by Dominic and Benedict whose priories and abbeys still freely elect their own leaders.

IX

AID TO CATHOLIC SCHOOLS

I

At the time of the first Vatican Council, Archbishop Ullathorne wrote Newman that many of the bishops were anxious to reaffirm the principle that laymen should take second place to clergy in theological discussions.[1] Ullathorne had the doctrinal pronouncements of Veuillot, Acton, and W. G. Ward in mind, but he was interested above all in maintaining that distinction between functions in the Church which had been obscured by the agitation for and against the proclamation of infallibility. It is regrettable that a similar distinction could not be invoked in the recurrent debates on federal aid to parochial schools or to parochial school children. Since the very existence of the Catholic educational system is based on a collective prudential judgment by the entire Catholic community — and not merely by the episcopate — and since there is nothing sacrosanct about the survival of this particular type of educational organization, and since, furthermore, the role of ecclesiastical authority in the formal schooling of the child is mediated by the parents on whom this task devolves directly, it would have been juridically justifiable and politically expedient to have had the laity assume the dominant part in initiating the necessary action, and in carrying it through according to the lights of their own state.

The hierarchy, of course, must speak out; but they must speak as informed advisors rather than as churchmen enunciating decrees. That in some cases they have chosen the latter course, that in some cases they have implied the possibility of using

---

[1] Cuthbert Butler, *The Vatican Council*, I, p. 216.

their ecclesiastical power to launch reprisals against the proponents of federal aid to public education exclusively, is at the
least — given the state of public opinion in America today —
imprudent, and at the most an exorbitant extension of their
office. One does not assert this distinction of functions in order
to dislodge the barbs of those critics who castigate the Catholic
community as monolithic; it is certainly not a question of giving
the lie to Protestants and Others, but rather of simply maintaining
that equilibrium in our religious structure which is implicit in
the very notion of a hierarchy and a laity. However, I do not
think one should be too hasty in assigning episcopal directives —
as has been done by much of the popular press as recently as
fall of 1967 in the New York controversy over state school aid —
as the motive for the obstructing tactics of Catholic legislators.
In fact, anyone who reads the speeches of some of these legislators cannot but be impressed by their reasoned character and
their national rather than their sectarian tone, as for instance
the following from congressman James J. Delaney:

The existence of a free society is conditioned upon the existence
of unshackled individuals with differing views and different approaches.
Diversity is the quintessence of democracy. Uniformity is the hall-
mark of totalitarianism. . . . The tragedy here lies in the fact that
proponents of strictly public aid rely upon extraconstitutional slogans
that have no relation to the real issue at hand — and that issue is
whether we shall maintain in our national life that measure of diversity
which is so essential to democratic survival.[2]

Statements such as this illustrate, as do scores of speeches of
other Catholic lawmakers, that political exigencies, not ecclesiastical urging, dictate their position on aid to education.

The argument for the creation of a truly pluralist educational
order is unquestionably the strongest which can be brought forth
in defense of the general Catholic position. Pro or con views
based on constitutional law are usually of secondary value, and
occasionally of little merit at all, save in the scoring of debating
points. And those Catholics who argue so eloquently and per-
suasively on constitutional grounds must admit in the end that
the question of precedents is itself so controverted, and that
precedents have so often been completely reversed — as in the

---

[2] *Congressional Record*, August 10, 1961, A6257.

case of "separate but equal" facilities — that any decision on constitutionality must await the action of the Court on a bill which has already been passed. Antecedent to the passage of such a bill, those who advocate federal aid, whether direct or indirect to the school or to the pupil, must establish their claims on a present need of the society and on a living tradition of political science, rather than on a constitutional or legalistic literalism.

Of course, to say that views based on constitutional law are usually of secondary value is not to say they are insignificant — or tertiary. They are simply not primary, even when they are of great importance. What is primary here is the ethos which generated these laws, and in which they find their true meaning. It is this ethos, which in our polity is personalistic, that has been responsible for every beneficial modification in our legal system concerning civil liberties.

Because the legal arguments have thus far proved inconclusive, it is necessary to move back to this personalistic basis if any progress is to be made in the discussion of aid to education. Nor should there be any sharp conflict between these two approaches since it is precisely this creative interplay between the primary datum (the ethical tenor of a society) and the secondary data (the positive prescriptions) that denominates the field of politics as a prudential area, as *jurisprudence*, and that preserves it from degenerating into a sterile positivism. Thus it is obvious that it was mainly the higher ethical principle, rather than the legal argumentation of the NAACP attorneys, which brought about the reversal of the "separate but equal" decision. True, the legal arguments are of great importance. But a constitutional lawyer without a sense of the ethos of our society is somewhat like a theologian without faith: he becomes only a manipulator of abstractions and a technician of the text.

Thus it is fundamentally the requirements of a genuine pluralism that dissipate the arguments of those opposed to federal aid to private schools. No one will question that with the gradual secularization of public schools over the past hundred years there has been a drift toward an enforced orthodoxy, and that notwithstanding the guarantees of local control and the statements of such professional bodies as the American Council on Education that, "we reject secularism as a philosophy of life," this tendency toward uniformity is going to continue. The only way in which this drift can be effectively thwarted is by the development of vigorous private school systems. It is true that one must take into account the earnestness with which the majority of teachers in public schools attempt to assert in their teaching spiritual values while avoiding any kind of sectarian instruction; but it is equally true that despite the goodwill of these teachers, a common unitary standard does tend to prevail in public education, and that this standard is gradually smothering the seeds of any germinating pluralism.

This is apparent in the very terms used to decry the Catholic school system: the most common criticism is that it is divisive. And given the present fabric of our society, one can only agree. But every division involves a duality, and it can be said with equal accuracy that the same charge could be brought against the public school. If we continue the present line of growth we are going to have two immense educational orders in America, each of which will create its own climate of ideas and its own tenor of attitudes, and each of which will find it increasingly difficult to communicate with the other. In the future even more than in the present we shall have not a pluralist but a dualist society, and we shall encounter more and more the kind of venomous eruptions which exploded throughout France after passage of the Barangé law in 1951, and which have burst to the surface periodically in the public life of Belgium and Holland.

But this dualist body politic is precisely what every major document in our social theory has been framed to avoid. Disraeli's "two nations" and Lincoln's "half slave and half free" both describe political monstrosities, and contradict that ideal of this society — best outlined in the Federalist Papers — which was to prevent the formation of preponderant power groups. This ideal has been preserved in our political parties through the creative tension within them of their conservative and liberal wings; but this ideal is on the way to being dissolved in factious fury with the present controversy over public and private education.

Unfortunately the phrase "private education" is very close to being a euphemism for "Catholic education." And this points up a social evil which ought to be corrected not in the name of denominationalism, but in the name of pluralism. What is basic, if we are going to preserve the kind of polity envisioned embryonically in the writings of the founders of the nation, is the development through public money by sectarian groups of educational systems which can meet the requirements of the community as a whole. This would in no way abridge the Constitution, since what that document was concerned with was "an establishment" of religion: a term which meant a century and a half ago what it still means in England today: an official religion of the land.

Professor Oscar Handlin has inquired as to "who is to set the standard of adequacy?"[3] for schools that will receive government assistance. His response was, regrettably, neither very comprehensive nor very perceptive. He answered his own question: "Already the states have gone far, too far, in establishing requisites of instruction; and the resultant damage has only been mitigated by inefficiencies in enforcement," and in another essay he was even more explicit: "There can only be one answer — the government."[4] This does not seem a readily verifiable statement, since it is a matter of record that the criteria established by the various professional bodies throughout the country have been much more rigorous than those defined by state boards of public instruction. But why exhume the ubiquitous monster of state control? The obvious answer to Professor Handlin's question is that the regional accrediting agencies, composed for many years now of educators from all types of schools, public, parochial, private-neutral, and private-sectarian, constitute the best qualified organizations to assess the academic merits of a school. This is done in England where the Education Ministry examines neither students nor teachers, but leaves these tasks to nine groups of professional educators associated with various normal colleges and with the universities.

It is in the detailed articulation of a program for establishing a large number of religiously oriented school systems that we have much to learn from the experience of other countries. In Germany, Belgium, and Holland, where there are two major denominations, and in those five of the ten Canadian provinces

---

[3] The Catholic World (July, 1961).
[4] Commentary (July, 1961).

— with the exception of Newfoundland — which provide tax support for confessional schools, the situation is so different from that in this country, with our much wider diversity of religious bodies, that it could have little bearing on any practical scheme for fostering denominational education here. But in Great Britain, where there is a comparable range of religious affiliation, formulas have been worked out that might partially guide us in correcting the current maladjustment. This is one of the lessons brought out with great thoroughness and exhaustive scholarship in Benjamin Sacks' *The Religious Issue in the State Schools of England and Wales: 1902–1914*.[5] What is particularly evident from a reading of this book is the intense effort on the part of the British government — the government of a country where there has been "an establishment" of religion — to assure all religious groups within the nation of the type of education they required. The problem in England and Wales was to guarantee flourishing sectarian and private schools for those who could sustain them with government assistance, and to make such schools an integral part of the community where they were located.

Since Catholic education in this country is so firmly established that it would be impossible for various other denominations to develop their own systems proportionate to the needs of their members, some method will have to be devised to achieve parity. Professor Sacks points out that in England and Wales an equitable arrangement was attempted in the nineteenth century by allowing the religious bodies a period of grace in which to build schools in deficient districts at the expense of the State. But thereafter national grants for construction would cease, although annual appropriations for maintenance would continue to be dispensed. The situation in England after the last war is even more pertinent to the issues flowing from the type of nationwide sectarian educational scheme desiderated above. For the reconstruction of schools the government was to bear the entire cost if the school would consent to be managed by a board, two-thirds of whose members were appointed by the local authority and one-third by the religious denomination;

---

[5] Albuquerque, 1961.

the state would bear only one-half the cost of reconstruction if two-thirds of the places on the board were held by members of the religious denomination. These are not necessarily financial arrangements that could be applied directly in this country; but they indicate the type of adjustment that can be made if there is a sincere search for a broad national policy, and a sincere effort to constrict prejudice. However, because in the immediate present there is only a limited amount of money available, whether through state or federal agencies, and since Catholics already have a well-established school system, one would hope that they would dismiss their current claims with a view to freeing by such a gesture — and it would be only a gesture, though a gesture of great significance — funds for other denominational schools.

It has been understandably difficult for non-Catholics to avoid the impression in recent years that Catholics — at least as their views have been represented by certain of their spokesmen — are willing to jeopardize any government assistance to education if their own schools are not included. To the degree that this attitude stems from purely religious considerations it reveals a culpable prejudice against public education, and an inability to transcend sectarian loyalties and make sacrifices for the common good. In the face of such narrow intransigence it would seem naïve to expect from Catholics the type of abnegation I have spoken of earlier, in which they would temporarily set aside their claims in order that other denominations might develop their own schools. But it should be remembered that the statements threatening extinction for any federal aid bill have not necessarily represented the views of Catholics as a whole, nor have they been the product of any profound political philosophy of pluralism. In this latter sense they are the pardonable effort of one of many pressure-groups to lobby for its own special interests. Such a strategy may be inexpedient and imprudent — emanating as it does from a segment of society which is demanding public moneys on the basis of the common good — but it is not outside the norms of sanctioned procedure for influencing legislation.

Looking in retrospect at recent controversies over aid to private schools, one feels that both sides could have been more candid.

Catholic educators could have acknowledged that they were willing to give up some autonomy, that they were, for instance, open to allowing a board of education or of lay trustees a greater voice in the academic affairs of their institutions. They could have acknowledged, at least intra-murally, that the financial difficulties of Catholic schools were to some degree the result of causes which utterly eclipsed the economic sphere. Thus the major critical area in Catholic education is the teacher shortage; Catholic school superintendents are willing to accept loans or grants for construction and other needs, largely because they know that money will thus be freed for salaries. But this personnel problem is related directly and inescapably to the shortage of religious vocations, and can only be adequately understood in the light of those imponderable factors which may inhibit the spiritual and liturgical life of the entire Catholic community. It might even be suggested that the present agitation for federal aid on the part of a growing and economically flourishing Catholic population is indicative of a decline in religious vigor from that earlier period when Catholic schools were founded by an impoverished minority, and when religious vocations were proportionate to their needs. No one has a right to oversimplify extremely complicated sociological realities, but it should go without saying that certain aspects of Catholic social life are rooted in the spiritual rather than in the temporal order.

On the other hand, it would have cleared the air if non-Catholics had acknowledged that to a considerable degree their opposition was motivated not by constitutional concerns, but by a prejudice — whether in part justifiable or not — against the allegedly growing power of Catholicism. When the National Lutheran Council, meeting in February, 1960, passed a resolution that "Government aid for the construction of church-operated schools at the elementary level is clearly a form of tax support for sectarian instruction," the impression to be created was that these particular churches were concerned primarily with questions of legality. This may be the case since on neither side of the controversy are the issues simply black or white — but I think such seemingly patriotic admonitions may be understood more fully in the light of a book by A. H. Jahsmann, *What's Lutheran in Education?* The author notes that many "Lutherans frankly fear the additional power that state support of church schools would give to the Roman Catholic Church in America and the problem of preventing this aggressive church from demanding more than its share of state support."[6]

A similar fear underlies the recurrent analogies that have obscured this question. For example, Leo Pfeffer, General Counsel for the American Jewish Congress, draws a much-quoted parallel with the demand for federal aid by Catholics and problems arising in certain communities over water fluoridation:

> It would undoubtedly be a great expense for Christian Scientists living in communities with a fluoridated water supply to purchase unfluoridated water as required by their consciences. Yet I have not come across a single report of a demand by Christian Scientists that the government give them money so that they can buy such water and thus be economically able to exercise their freedom of religion.[7]

The analogy falters on two points. First, although it has been maintained by conservative political theorists, Friedrich Hayek for example, that private agencies are as able to provide individual localities with such services as water and sewerage disposal, the generally accepted assumption is that the local or the national government can more effectively preside over the execution of such necessary common tasks. But — and this is the cardinal issue — no such assumption in favor of public education over private education has ever been underwritten or implied by our laws. Second, most communities charge a fee for the particular service rendered; this fee is not a tax, but the purchase price of a commodity over the sale of which the government exercises a monopoly. If I as a farmer prefer to generate my own electric power rather than purchase it from the government or from a private corporation, or if I as a Christian Scientist pump water from my own well, I can hardly be expected to honor a bill from some third party. Of course, I may be indirectly taxed for such governmental services; but Catholics are not complaining that some of their money goes to support the public schools; they are grieved that none of it goes to their own schools.

---

[6] St. Louis, 1960, p. 142.
[7] *Current History* (August, 1961).

If Mr. Pfeffer — who also narrates the even more preposterous example of Jehovah Witnesses demanding that the government print their propaganda — is not simply juggling parables for the entertainment of his sympathizers, he ought to follow out the implication of his analogy and maintain, for instance, that in a community where ninety percent of the property tax goes for support of schools, the Catholic is justified in using a portion of this money to "buy" the kind of schooling he prefers. The sad truth is that Mr. Pfeffer's fables presume that private schools are not really schools at all — fortunately whether they are or they are not is a determination to be made by educators, not by constitutional lawyers.

An illustration more enlightening than Mr. Pfeffer's might run as follows. If a broader compulsory medical aid bill than the one we now have is passed, and a Christian Scientist were taken ill, the courts might uphold the state's refusal to pay for his visit to a practitioner on the grounds that by common consensus the ministrations of the practitioner were not comparable to those of a doctor of medicine. Although the individual who is ill may subjectively be convinced that the benefits to be derived from visiting a practitioner are greater than those to be derived from visiting a doctor, the objective norm of the community would probably say they are not. Now Catholics have not asked that the private institutions which they finance, and which they — through a peculiarly Catholic accommodation of the word — call "schools," should be supported by public moneys; they have maintained that any objective standard used to define a school should be the norm for all institutions claiming that title. Catholics are willing to have their schools conform to whatever requirements are imposed by the various regional accrediting agencies or by the state boards of education. Catholics view their institutions as schools, as schools with an added element — as schools in which religion is an active principle; they believe that this enhances rather than negates their character as schools — and this belief far from being subjective has been statistically certified in Joseph H. Fichter's *Parochial School,* and in Peter and Alice Rossi's parallel study.[8]

---

[8] Notre Dame, 1958; *Daedalus* (Spring, 1961).

One could extend the analogy with a medical aid bill yet further; if I am ill I can buy a bottle of snake oil and demand that the government reimburse me; I can consult a medical doctor, or I can avail myself of the services of an osteopath. The only role of the government is to decide, by accepting the judgments of qualified experts, which of these agents or instruments conduces to health. Mr. Pfeffer's imagery would pair the Catholic educational institution with a case of Hadocol — this is not the kind of case one would expect an eminent lawyer such as Mr. Pfeffer to be handling.

I I

The key concept in the burgeoning folklore of ecumenism is "dialogue." This is a usable term, but it is beginning to assume those iconic properties which usually accompany the reifying of an abstraction; it tends to represent a kind of shamanist sacrament, that says what it works and works what it says, in the mystique of inter-confessional and public relations; and it may soon be freighted with so much imagery that its mere invocation will be enough to separate the good from the bad. All of this is by way of noting that the social accretions are obscuring the reality and that we are now so habituated to discussing "the dialogue," that we often overlook the fact that it exists not as an attainment but as a desideratum; and that rather than talking dialogue, we are usually just talking about it. For, though it is true that on a highly refined level of strictly theological discussion some genuine interchange does exist, its influence generally has not been widely felt. It is a regrettable and melancholy truth that socially and politically we are not yet entirely removed from the era of nativist suspicions so that the difference between the APA and the POAU is mainly abecedarian — and one's initial impression that they may differ turns out in the end to be merely the impression of an initial.

The encounter with the other, the dialogue, is realized on the plane of being; we are still on the plane of doing and making. Dialogue takes place at the summit of the pyramid of reality;

we are presently at its base, in the realm of method, technique, and device. And there is a great deal to be done by way of clearing away the brambles and undergrowth at the foot of this seven-storey mountain before we shall reach that garden-state where the lion and the lamb, or the hind and the panther, may lie down together.

In the context of the school aid controversy we seriously need a new vocabulary, one less loaded with the petrifactions of fantasy, if we are going to examine this issue with any kind of clarity. The old concepts have become so abused, so enervated, or so encrusted with the detritus of dead debates that they are no longer serviceable. Catholics, particularly of the *Triumph* mentality, have not yet completely renounced such loaded phrases as "Godless schools" or "double taxation," while many non-Catholics continue to employ such irrelevant figures as that of the "wall" of separation or "divisive education." Purifying the language of the tribe, which happens to be the language we all use, is not easy; the noblest of terms have become ambiguous and they are often the vehicles of conscious or unconscious prejudice.

To say that there is prejudice at play in the dispute over federal aid to church-related schools is not to indulge in name-calling; it is to recognize a fact of political life. Catholics are not all exercised over the national failure to pay homage to the principles of distributive justice, nor are non-Catholics all incensed over constitutional infringements. Nonetheless it is true, and for probably theological reasons alone, that Catholics generally tend to rely more on a living tradition of political ideology, and non-Catholics more on the written word of the law. Thus, some of the comments by opponents of aid to the confessional school leave one with the impression that they believed they were in the midst of a new — though verbal — gunpowder plot aimed at blowing up the metaphoric wall of separation. The fact is that many of the more impassioned and frenetic separatists are destroying their own vaunted defenses by overextending them and raising them too high. The wall is becoming too long to man, the ramparts too difficult to garrison, and if it falls it will be from its own excessive weight.

Conversely, it seems probable that the current solicitude for pluralism in some Catholic quarters has been dictated largely by expedience. Ten years ago the *Our Sunday Visitor* syndicate of diocesan newspapers was equating pluralism with doctrinal relativism and syncretism; but with the advent of the school-aid crisis, articles began to appear in that publication on the rights of Catholic schools to government support, bearing such titles as "Pluralism and Parochial Schools."[9] The conversion has been dramatic: what the editors took up and read, we shall perhaps never know — though there are many who will speculate.

All displays of excessive self-interest represent abuses, but they are abuses that must be candidly acknowledged if they are to be uprooted. However, it should also be recognized that there are many Catholics who are opposed to any such practices as Bible reading in the public schools, or to the erection of religious symbols in public buildings, and who are as firmly committed to the Constitutional principle of separation as their most enlightened fellow citizens. Similarly it should be emphasized that on the part of these Catholics their attachment to pluralism is free from all strategic or tactical interests. Nor is this surprising since the Church also reflects a pluralist order, each diocese being an *ecclesia* within itself. The alleged monolith of Catholicism turns out to be a mosaic, and Catholics are less startled than non-Catholics that the late Archbishop of St. Louis and the present Archbishop of Boston have expressed views on federal aid radically different from those of, e.g., the late Cardinal Spellman.

Not only is the Catholic as devoted to the principles of pluralism as any other citizen, he is also just as willing to apply them to concrete issues. Pluralism is a position that we must all subscribe to, whether as individuals it affects us favorably or not. Although in the controversy over aid to education it is probable that the fundamental personalism of our political order will redound ultimately to the advantage of church-related schools, on the other hand, this same political doctrine will frequently curb or restrain Catholics in other aspects of their institutional life. For example, it is perfectly justifiable for a non-Catholic patient to decry the refusal of a Catholic hospital, which re-

---

[9] February 25, 1962.

ceives public moneys, to perform an abortion when this is requested within the limits of the law for medical reasons, and when it would be unreasonably difficult to obtain it elsewhere. The hospital authorities can clearly assert, provided this involves no indirect coercion, their reprobation of any such practice, but unless they are willing to reject all government support, it is difficult to see how their refusal can be viewed as other than a violation of the spirit if not the letter of the Bradfield v. Roberts decision which constitutionalized public funds for religious hospitals.

Unfortunately, both Catholics and non-Catholics have often failed to grasp the pragmatic values of pluralism as they affect elementary and secondary education. We are justly proud in America of our universities which, in contrast to our grade and high schools, have preserved their individual standards in the face of political and popular threats or blandishments. But there is intrinsically very little which is more conducive to non-conformity in college teaching than in teaching on the lower levels; and anyone familiar, for example, with the state of many German universities after World War I and the uniformity which prevailed among the *Gelehrtenstand*, with its ready acquiescence in the goals of the Third Reich, must recognize that our great private universities have safeguarded that freedom which has partially eroded in secondary and elementary education because for the most part they are completely self-sufficient and independent of one another and of the state: they constitute a truly pluralist society. This impregnability to external attack, characteristic of our privately endowed colleges and universities, has so set the tone in higher education that even state universities have refused to abdicate their privileges before arbitrary decisions of local legislative bodies.

I have already set forth in the preceding section of this chapter some reasons for believing that the requirements of a genuine pluralism dissipate many of the arguments of those opposed to federal aid to private schools. However, I have also suggested that Catholics ought not to press their current claim for aid, and that this renunciation should be viewed not as an adroit expedient for assuring in the future what could probably never be attained in the present, but rather as an indication of their willingness to free government funds for other denominational schools. The pluralist principle demands that we break the present line of development which will culminate in two vast educational enterprises, the public and the parochial, and that we seek instead to construct an educational order which will truly reflect the various religious and moral commitments in our society. To avoid the disruptive strife that periodically bursts out in France, Belgium, and Holland we must move away from the accelerating dualism of the last four decades, and look toward the day when every religious sect and every moral or ethical group will maintain through governmental support its own schools. With such highly diversified educational systems, paralleling the public school system, we would have the social instruments for realizing within the framework of a single and unified tradition a multiplicity of opposing and conforming views, the common refraction of which would color the whole of our national life.

These recommendations after their original publication were stigmatized as "utterly impractical" by some observers.[10] But they have not proved impractical in certain Canadian provinces or in England and Wales. The multiplicity of denominations raises problems, but they are problems that are entirely secondary, entirely in the order of technique. In fact, there is no reason why the government should not support any school, no matter what splinter confessional group, no matter what minor sect, no matter what store-front cult may have established it, provided its faculties and curriculum conform to the standards of approved accrediting associations. We need, then, to foster institutions bearing names like the Cardinal Stritch College and the Bob Jones University, and we need to foster at all levels of education views as variant as those represented by such schools.

It is difficult to see why formulas could not be worked out with a view to the ultimate practical realization of this ideal. Guided in part by the standards defined in England after World War II, one might suggest, for example, that the state could initially pay two-thirds of the cost of construction for new schools in districts where a given segment of the

---

[10] *Commonweal* (March 2, 1962).

population indicated both a need for its own school and a willingness to provide one-half of the operating budget after completion. Since in the next ten years the potential high school population will increase by over forty percent, the obvious area for beginning the development of denominational schools would be on the secondary level. It is probable that, given such population growth, this would entail neither the closing of any existing public schools nor their transfer to sectarian control; but in the latter event, those who would argue that this might cause friction in a community could bear in mind that certain church school buildings would necessarily also be neutralized. The pluralist principle would require sacrifices on both sides. Thus if the sampling by Professor Dierenfield of Macalaster College is accurate — and it does generally appear to have been sufficiently broad in scope to allow for reasonably certain conclusions — some of the nearly eight percent of the two thousand school districts surveyed, in which church buildings are used for public school purposes, would probably experience a reversion of facilities from ecclesiastical to civil authorities.

The schema above is purely tentative and exploratory, but it would, no matter how amended, have consequences beneficial both to the nation as a whole and to the local community. Catholic schools would have to conform in the requirements of the curriculum and in the preparation of teachers, to the standards of some authorized board. (Such a board need not be an adjunct of the federal government, but instead could be a regional body modelled on or derived from the present accrediting agencies.) This would free the school from the clerical hegemony which now prevails, and which often frustrates any attainment of excellence by a faculty whose leaders — the local pastor — have no professional training or preparation for their academic roles. From the viewpoint of all schools, including neutral schools, each individual institution would be more responsive to the needs of the group which it served; and in place of the general lay indifference, about which so many public school administrators have complained, there would inevitably develop a sense of personal engagement with the work of the institution. Each school would be the result of the free vote of the parents, and it would therefore be much more representative of their vision and stance than are many of the present totally colorless public and parochial schools. Finally — and from the viewpoint of Roman Catholics, the most burdensome proposal of all — as I mentioned above, since in the present climate of obsession with victory in Vietnam, there will be only limited funds available for the achievement of such a goal, Catholics should dismiss their present claims with a view to freeing public moneys for the other denominational groups.

All of this may seem utterly utopian — but then so were social security, the eight-hour work day, medicare, and the more recent disavowal of segregation as a national policy. However, such an educational ideal remains at the top of the pyramid: like the dialogue it will be realized only after a great deal of mental underbrush has been cleared away. And it is the main purpose of the conclusion of this chapter to indicate certain areas where Catholics can contribute to this common national ascesis.

It is not necessary to be concerned with those Catholics who candidly believe that federal aid to public schools exclusively represents a dagger at the heart of the parochial school system, nor with those who assume that it is prejudice that motivates most non-Catholics in their opposition to assistance to church-related schools. These are the views of the extremist fringes, and they have their counterpart within the non-Catholic community; one simply expects that the two antagonist views will, in virtue of their exaggerations, cancel each other out. But there is a large central domain where men of reason ought to be able to meet — regrettably, up to now the meetings have not been very fruitful. It should be said frankly that many of the participants on both sides do not seem to have approached the conference table with the requisite purity of vision and sympathy to grasp the opposing point of view. And one may hope that the ACLU or the American Jewish Congress would broaden the perspectives of such dialecticians as Oscar Handlin and Leo Pfeffer, while the present chapter would point out some of the flaws in the argumentation of many equally sincere and able Catholic polemicists. It is only after we have purified both our vision and our language that we will be able to approach the summit for the dialogue.

I have already referred to the hasty espousal of pluralism by

Catholics who previously have been blandly content with what they seemed to view as our monomorphic society. Equally as incomprehensible is the sudden concern now evidenced by some Catholics over State control of public education. It is rather difficult to understand the "creeping socialism" argument embraced by the many political leaders favorable to Church-school aid who criticized that frequently misinterpreted statement of the Department of HEW, "A Federal Education Agency for the Future." Since such an agency would have been necessary if the federal government entered actively into the support of schools, and since such politicians had argued eloquently and soundly for broadening this support to embrace church-related education (which would inevitably have made this agency all the more imperative), the impression was understandably created that they were simply kicking up dust to obscure the issue, and thus interdict passage of any bill which ran counter to their own proposals. This equivocal position tended to reinforce the popular notion — which would otherwise have been viewed as journalistic myth — that it was ecclesiastical prodding rather than an awareness of the diverse needs of our society which dictated the position of many Catholic politicians on federal aid.

But though one may question the ambiguity of such political pronouncements, they remain the personal opinions of individual Catholics, and can hardly be said to represent authoritative views. One is, however, a bit dismayed when eminent ecclesiastics indicate that they are opposed to federal aid to public schools on similar apparently detached political grounds. Thus the Coadjutor Archbishop of Baltimore declared in 1962, "that there has been no conclusive demonstration of the need of federal aid to public schools generally. On the contrary, there are clear indications that there is no such general need. There have been claims made by interested individuals and organizations committed not only to federal aid but also federal control; but there has been no clear, objective demonstration of the truth of these claims." This is a statement which could be made in good conscience by any number of conservative political scientists, and though one may disagree with its bias, it can hardly be said to reflect a completely untenable view. However, this altruistic and selfless concern for the common good becomes suspect when one recalls that this was not the utterance of a private person, but of a Roman Catholic archbishop speaking not as one citizen to another, but as the designated preacher at a public liturgical function.

In like manner it is no contribution to the approaching dialogue on this question for *Triumph*-style Catholics to equate public education with "secularism." (This, too, is one of those over-burdened terms that needs purifying.) In fact, the secular school no more need foster secularism than the parochial school need foster "parochialism." When either does, it is an example of the abuse of a good thing — and this abuse never takes away subsequent right use. The public school must be a neutral school dedicated to the principles of a natural humanism, as these principles have been partially exemplified both in the tenor of the many delicate and finely balanced decisions of the Supreme Court, and in such statements as that of the American Council on Education that "we reject secularism as a philosophy of life." I think it is a serious error to say with Mr. William Whalen in the *Sunday Visitor* article cited above, that: "Of the four major commitments in American society — Protestantism, Catholicism, Judaism, and Secularism — the State has favored one, namely, Secularism." To the degree that this is so, it is to be as much deplored as such other violations of the law as the distributing of Bibles or the conducting of religious exercises in public schools.

Finally, one is with difficulty impressed by the persuasiveness of those who maintain that patrons of Church-related schools suffer under a nefarious double standard of taxation. These proponents of federal aid have sketched a dilemma which runs as follows: if Catholic schools are strictly religious centers, then tuition fees should be tax deductible as contributions to religious undertakings; if they are strictly educational, then they should receive the same support as public educational institutions. But in either case there must be some kind of governmental alleviation of the present burden imposed on Catholics. This kind of over-simplification tends to reduce the pluralist conception to a monism, to an either-or proposition. And in mere matter of fact, all church-related agencies, including parochial schools, do enjoy a number of tax advantages precisely because they are religious in character. Similarly, Catholics as parents are allowed the same deductions for dependents as other citizens. The type of tax adjustment for religious institutions and for the rearing of children which has been made throughout our history, and which has been rigorously preserved by the decisions of the Court, indicates an implicit recognition that pluralism involves a both/ and commitment. It is no more a question of separation or unity, of the law or the ethos of society, than in theology it is a question of the Scriptures or tradition. These polarities are fused in that dynamic tension, which in the political sphere we call "pluralism."

Pluralism is derived from personalism, it is derived from the classic notion that man, and consequently his society, is constituted by an intensive interplay between his spirit and his matter, between his personality and his individuality, between his freedom and his limitations. In certain periods of history, before a national spirit has matured, the emphasis will be on the principles of limitation and on legalistic literalism: in this case, separatism as viewed as the best pragmatic policy for guaranteeing the best education for the largest numbers. But, when a nation has reached its full stature in its people, when the various communities within it are capable of exercising their freedom, when most of the constraints of economic and social deprivation have been transcended, then the more spiritual and therefore more fluid principle of pluralism will become regnant, and this principle will subsume and give meaning to all inferior principles, including the principle of separation. It is now apparent that we are approaching that moment in our history, and that no citizens serve the common good by assuming a narrow unitary position.

X

TOWARD A THEOLOGY
OF ANIMALS

I

The mind of every man experiences some great crux when attempting to understand the Christian synthesis. For Newman it was the New Testament teaching on eternal punishment; for William George Ward it was the scholastic doctrine on predestination; for scores of parents in the early Church, one assumes it was the theological notion that the unbaptized were damned; and for scores of parents in our time it may very well be the dubious theory of a limbo for unbaptized infants. But for many others, who simply reject the mechanistic conception of the *communio sanctorum* on which the limbo theory is based, it will be the problem raised by animal suffering.

These latter believe, on good theological grounds, that all the agonies of an innocent child dying are requited and find meaning in the next world; but traditionally the painful death of an animal has been regarded as having no meaning in itself; it is only a kind of symbol for man, a symbol of the truth that he should willingly accept necessary suffering without complaint — after the manner of the "dumb brute." But if this were the entire truth one could not help but think it a cruel symbol that some kind of vengeful God had offered to mankind. For of course the animal is a symbol — but then so is man himself, plus something more. And it is this "something more" that theology has left undefined with regard to animal creation.

The living animal is a twofold symbol reminding man, first, of Eden garden and of that integrity and purity that he lost there. Even more, the animal is a symbol of man's undefiled image; for Adam's act of naming the animals was not an assertion of his dominion over them. This naming represented rather Adam's candid companionship with that aspect of creation which had been created in his image even as he had been created in the image of God. And hence the friendship of the great saints with the animals: the great saints preached to them, and the animals in the act of comprehending such "sermons" comprehended themselves and realized through the saints — the men most akin to Adam before the fall — their place in a divine economy which ordinary man has not been able to grasp.

But if the animal is a symbol of what creation was in its state of innocence, he is also a symbol of what man is now in his state of estrangement. The piteous glance of the animal — of which no one has written more eloquently than Buber[1] — comes from the fact that the animal cannot quite respond to the *sursum corda* of his being, from the fact that he cannot quite communicate his very selfness to another. The animal symbolizes then, simply because of his incapacity to release his spirit from captivity, the fractioned condition of fallen man. For the animal is trapped in a way that man is not, and therefore experiences in a way that man cannot — blindly and by the most tortuously indirect reflection — the excruciating tension of the spirit-matter construct. And thus because the animal's eyes express the frustration of a spirit too diminished, too powerless to penetrate its material envelope we rightly speak only of the tragic "glance" of the animal and not of its "gaze": the emergence of spirit in the animal is a momentary event, without transforming power and without endurability. But in this ontological sadness, in this strain of his nature the animal speaks silently of the groaning and travailing of the whole of an expectant creation. And so it was no exaggeration for Matthew Arnold to write:

> That liquid, melancholy eye,
> From whose pathetic, soul-fed springs
> Seemed surging the Virgilian cry,
> The sense of tears in mortal things.[2]

---

[1] Martin Buber, *I and Thou* (New York, 1958), pp. 96–99.
[2] "Geist's Grave."

Yet having recognized the wealth of all of this symbolic significance, it is still difficult to find much meaning in the death throes of the animal. One might say in palliation of this seeming horror that animals do not have authentic self-consciousness, and that their sufferings, therefore, are greatly diminished by contrast to those that the human person undergoes; granted in part — though we are embracing a possibility (lack of animal self-awareness) to erase a certitude (the pain of dying) — because no matter how muted, there is still some suffering. And any suffering which is utterly without significance implies a world in which a meaningless situation takes place, and this is a denial of God.

There is some hint of a solution to this problem in that obscure passage, already alluded to, from the epistle to the Romans where St. Paul proclaims that "creation itself also will be delivered from its slavery to corruption into freedom of the glory of the sons of God." Almost all exegetes agree that "creation" here refers to the physical world and to the animals that dwell in it. But the text remains baffling, and can perhaps only be understood by reading it in the light of the message of the great pauline visionary of our time, Teilhard de Chardin; and for that reason it is also somewhat consoling because it hints at an explanation for the one dominant mystery in the physical universe, the pains of animals. St. Paul's proclamation suggests that even animals share in the redemption; which means in turn, that they must also share in the parousia and in the final renewal of this world. Every creature according to its own nature, inasmuch as it fulfills the will of God according to that nature (man freely moved by God, animals more unfreely) will then participate in the final consummation, though, as Karl Rahner says, "it staggers the imagination to conceive how."[3]

"Imagination" is the proper word here. For in the growing concern both within and without the Christian community over the pains of animals we are faced with one of those revolutions which sensibility often so successfully engenders in the face of abstract cerebration. In fact, a parallel could readily be drawn here with the change which sensibility — *non in dialectica* —

---

[3] *On the Theology of Death* (New York, 1961), p. 36.

wrought in the early Church when the notion that unbaptized children were damned was finally and definitively abandoned. For this reason such witnesses to the salvation of animals as Bishop Butler, Charles Kingsley, Cardinal Manning, Baron von Hügel, and C. S. Lewis, can be recognized as the prophets of a new but not unexpected development of Christian doctrine.

This growing dissatisfaction with the traditional Christian view of animals, both in and out of religious circles, stems almost entirely from the depths of sensibility and empathy which have been discovered by post-medieval man. For this reason the animal-welfare movement can be recognized as derivative of that common body of opinion which in recent centuries has brought about the amelioration of conditions among laborers and factory workers, the universal condemnation of slavery, the improvement of penitentiaries, the abolition or humanizing of various instruments for capital punishment, and virtually every other beneficial social reform.

Without oversimplifying needlessly it can nevertheless be affirmed that this emergence, or better, eruption, of a new dimension in human sympathy is the direct consequence of man's discovery of selfness, of his discovery that his dignity stems not from his place in society, not from his function in this or that office or work, not from his biological antecedents, but entirely from his own spiritual character. Lord Acton has traced this growing realization of personhood to the diffusion of the stoic writings in the late middle ages;[4] and it is a commonplace of historical knowledge that this realization culminated in what is ineptly termed "the romantic movement." It is not surprising then, that protestantism which represents this same romantic vision in the religious sphere, has traditionally been more sympathetic to humanistic reform movements than has Roman Catholicism.[5]

It would be an injustice to attempt to condense multifaceted and complex cultural and sociological tendencies into a single

---

[4] *Lectures on Modern History, op. cit.,* p. 73.

[5] Similarly it is not surprising that the theological *école romantique* of Tübingen, under the influence of Möhler, has come to be appreciated by Catholics only in this century.

linear evolution, or to attempt to write a philosophy of history in a few lines; but it is quite obvious that the discovery of selfness is the basic factor in the development of Western social consciousness. For social consciousness is engendered only to the degree that man comes to recognize his own personhood, his own interiority; and it is paradoxic but axiomatic that the subject only knows itself in knowing the object, while the object is only fully known in reflection on the subject.

This awareness of man's authentic humanness was inhibited by medieval culture both in its religious and its secular aspects (to the degree that they are discernible and separable), by such additional factors as the confinement of education to the clergy and nobility, the mechanistic *ex opere operato* conception of the sacraments and consequently though regrettably of the entire ecclesiastical structure, and finally by the intellectual inbreeding of all aristocratic closed societies, whether political, academic, or religious. All of these and many other influences made pre-reformation man a being who was defined fundamentally in terms of outwardness and exteriority. And it is because of this cultural ordination to the world of the objective that it is difficult to embrace either Christopher Dawson's notion of a Christian culture, or Karl Rahner's notion of a present-day diaspora. There never was a Christian culture, there was only a Christian carapace; and this, because Christianity implies above all not an adherence from without enforced by the physical pressures of a highly stratified society, but an inner acceptance of Christ. Without any sense of interiority such an acceptance is impossible.

These are necessarily loose generalizations, but their main drift is recognized as valid by virtually every historian of our time. And they serve to explain why on the grounds of a misconceived natural-law doctrine Christian bishops could defend slavery even in the nineteenth century, and, more pertinent to the present subject, they explain why even today Roman Catholics will defend vivisection on that same natural-law doctrine bolstered by citations from that pre-eminently medieval thinker, Thomas Aquinas. The truth is that here as in a number of other fields St. Thomas has only a historical significance, and that twentieth-century man is no more likely to be swayed by his opinion that

animals have absolutely no rights than by his notion that more
people are damned than saved, or that burning at the stake is
a permissible punishment for heresy.

In the broader conception of animality which modern man
possesses, it can certainly be affirmed that the animal has an
instinct for life, and that since this instinct by definition is a
drive for life without any termination — all animals fear extinction — it is a tendency toward continued living as such. The
very awareness the animal has of its own physical dimensions
and of the impingement of objects on its sensory apparatus constitutes a kind of "conscious" individuality, a kind of embryonic
personality. The animal's instinct for life, then, is a thrust
toward a condition in which the stimuli of pleasure shall be
permanent and those of pain annihilated; and this thrust would
seem to be the experience of the individual animal and not
of the species. Moreover, the animal does have a sense of im-
pending harm, does have an awareness of anticipated pain, and
the very awareness itself, no matter how vague, must be an
additional source of suffering which is entirely *non-physical*.

For that reason it would be deeply satisfying to the modern
mind, in whom empathy for the pains of others — whether persons or animals — has been much more thoroughly cultivated
than it could ever have been in the medieval world, if Roman
Catholic theological and philosophical manuals would consign
to the rubble of dead history the notion of *vis aestimativa*, and
instead treat of animal knowledge as inchoately spiritual, and
therefore as demanding for its subject correlative spiritual rights.
That is the clear meaning of the following lines by the priest-poet,
Henry Vaughan, on St. Paul's text from *Romans:*

> And do they so: have they a Sense
> Of ought but Influence?
> Can they their heads lift, and expect,
> And grone too? why th'Elect
> Can do no more: my volumes sed
> They wer all dull, and dead,
> They judg'd them senslesse, and their state
> Wholly Inanimate.
> Go, go; Seal up thy looks,
> And burn thy books.[6]

---

[6] "Rom. Cap. 8. ver. 19."

With theological and metaphysical wit Vaughan punned in the first line on the passage in which Christ explicitly affirmed God's concern for animal creation even though it neither reaps nor sows. And in the word play on ought-aught, he went even further to suggest that since the animal does have a sense of "ought," which implies obligation, then he is, like man, a kind of spiritual creature. This "oughtness" would require that the animal simply be what he is, as of course nothing else is possible. But is not that for man also the highest fulfillment of obligation and thus the highest form of prayer — simply to be what he is, to accept fully his creaturehood?

Thus there is an adequate basis for the elaboration of a theology of animals which would explicitly affirm their immortality. The doctrine would have to emphasize, first, the participation of the animal's spirit in the human spirit, even as the human spirit is a participation in God; and, second, the affinity of the animal body with the human body, and of the body of the latter with the body of the God-man. And as the human spirit is incomplete without its body, one would maintain that the animal spirit would also demand union with its body. This is simply to emphasize again that the central issue does not relate to any vaguely defined salvation of the species, but to the saving of the individual animal as such.

It is at this point that one can answer that question which seems to vex unduly those who do not see the immense symbolic value of a doctrine of reverence for life, and who seem to delight in inquiring about such matters as the fate of swarms of insects or of other lower forms of life. To the question of where one draws the line — bearing in mind that it is not for man to draw any such lines but only to attempt to satisfy his own confusion before mystery — it must be replied that one would imagine it to be drawn at the limits of flesh and blood. Great is the emphasis in the Christian revelation on the "body and blood of Christ," on that body and blood which was assumed precisely in order that a God might suffer. And it is because the animal can undergo his "passion" — in the root sense of the word — that he must share in the resurrection. One draws the line, then, at the lowest extremity of creatures who share in spirit and who are compounded of nerves, and blood.

Now if all of this may be maintained, one is well on the way to exiling to the dark chambers of the past — along with the history of bear-baiting and bullfighting, to say nothing of autos-da-fè — the monstrous scholastic notion that animals, like heretics, are to be treated as mere things. Any creature when it reaches the threshold of experiencing and anticipating pain possesses rights.

Some of this may sound exorbitant, but it at least moves one in the direction of explaining what in the traditional Christian worldview is simply left inexplicable. And it is at least a step toward a solution which finds some meaning in the otherwise meaningless suffering of animal creation.

We are in need of a broad-gauge sociology of religion. Such a sociology might help us know, for instance, to what extent national traits have been reflected in the various theological schools and have shaped theological opinion. It is obvious that a concern for animal life has been characteristic mainly of that Anglo-Saxon religious temper which, as Cardinal Newman stressed, is deeply rooted in the affective, the concrete, and the empiric, that is, in the terrestrial. Nor is it a mere matter of taste that led to the inclusion of two texts from English poets in the paragraphs above. Works on the pains of animals and on the meaning of animal creation almost constitute a genre in the English poetic tradition — one need think only of Vaughan, Blake, Coleridge, Arnold, Hodgson, Thomas, Monro, Stephens, and Wolfe. On the other hand, since the continental theological tradition is mainly Latin and speculative, it is not surprising that the mystery of animals has been virtually ignored by Catholic religious thinkers. And this, it may be suggested, is why when one looks at the major popular entertainment in those happy Iberian lands, which for centuries enjoyed the benefits of clerical tyranny, one is not always impressed by the impact of religion on the sanctification of man in his concrete, real condition.

Bullfighting must be viewed as a grave and intolerable immorality, and the assertion that it can be regarded as an esthetic enterprise is irrelevant: murder itself can be ritualized, as Kafka's "execution machine" would illustrate. What is even more perverse, and a grievous scandal, in these countries is the sanctioned torture of animals in conjunction with religious festivities. Although it took the Church centuries to forbid clerics to bear arms as professional soldiers, and although at the first Vatican Council Bishop Vérot of Florida, who wanted to have priests forbidden to hunt, was derided by his brethren,[7] nevertheless considerable progress has been made in the humanizing of institutional religion. And notwithstanding the fact that our zoos continue to enclose animals in cages that are only two or three times larger in dimension than the size of the beasts themselves, and that small wild animals are imprisoned without a mate for life in tiny glass cells where they have no contact with any living thing save for the daily insertion of a food tray — notwithstanding the fact that such immoralities continue to be perpetrated for the delight of the onlooking images of God — it nevertheless remains true that the more gross evils have gradually been eradicated. We don't bait bears, we don't fight cocks, we don't impale bulls, and even nonbrutalized slaughter-houses are replacing the vile abbatoirs of the past — at least in the non-Roman Catholic world.

All of this points up the significance of Joy Adamson's series on Elsa the lion. The popularity of these books — which counter the Disneyland conception of love for animals as primarily a juvenile virtue — indicates a radical change in the general sensibility. They constitute a Christian testimony of man's devotion to animals which is utterly remote from the complete indifference of many Roman Catholics as well as from the academic franciscanism of the defenders of "moderate" vivisection. *Forever Free*, like *Born Free* and *Living Free*, breathes the kind of piety we identify with Anglicanism at its best, and one may be pardoned for preferring this Joy with her religious naturalism to that galvanic virgin whose psychophysical contortings Bernanos portrayed. Joy Adamson and the growing school of contemporary writers to which she belongs seek to put together that divided image which the world of experience begets, and to tell us that the fearful symmetry of the tiger in the night was traced by the same hand that made the lamb. These books, like certain paintings of Chagall and Franz Marc, restore us for a time to that

---

[7] James J. Hennesey, S.J., *The First Council of the Vatican* (New York, 1963), p. 242.

garden state where the lion and the lamb lay down together .They are works of religion in the *deepest* sense.

It is here that any theology of animals must situate itself: in the tenable thesis that animals, like angels, explicitly share in our worship of God. They are a part of that liturgy which must be dearest to the Father if only because his Son when preparing for his redemptive mission, as St. Mark says, "lived among animals and was served by angels."

Any discussion on the theology of animals must broach that question of vivisection which shall be examined in greater detail in part two of this chapter. Many twentieth-century Christians, and recently even some Roman Catholics, have found it almost impossible to understand why the animal which — according to traditional opinion — has no other life can be forced to suffer in this its one life in order to extend or preserve that temporal life of man which in the Christian conception is merely the prelude to an eternal life. That is the larger premise on which many Christian antivivisectionists would base their argument. But even apart from specifically Christian considerations, it is difficult to find any ethical justification whatever for the infliction of needless pain on animals — how to define "needless pain" shall be taken up shortly. Certainly since animals exist for the good of man (but because of their rich participation in spirit that "good" is not to be understood as though they were primarily physical objects or mere things), even as man exists for the good of his fellow man, one may justify the necessary and painless killing of animals just as one might justify the necessary and painless killing of a murderously intent criminal. But in neither case could one on any grounds justify torture. Nor in the case of such a criminal could one argue that because he had abdicated his human rights it would therefore be licit to attempt medical experiments on his now "non-human" body. Furthermore, if it is reason that presumably distinguishes man from the animals, and if on the basis of that distinction vivisection is allowable, then it ought to be equally allowable to perform experiments on the permanently deranged. For certainly, one could say, the permanently insane may be adjudged to have no rights; they can neither contribute anything to the human community nor can they praise God through formal prayer — even when, like animal creation, they can praise God by their mere existence, by their lack of duplicity and by their innocence.

The alleged presence or absence of higher faculties in men and animals has no bearing on the question of vivisection as such. What is relevant is the fact that both men and animals are sentient, are capable of experiencing pain. There is no verifiably significant correlation between possession of reason and awareness of suffering; nor can we in the name of the first impose the second. What reason does give man is the power to tyrannize other creatures, the power to imagine that he shall be as God — that is, the power to deny his creaturehood, a denial which both Greek tragedy and the Old Testament teach degrades man to a condition lower than that of the brute. Since I shall discuss below the norms that should be established for all medical experimentation, I will not detail them here. But in the framework of the larger argument developed above, I would suggest the following as a summary rule for the determination of morally permissible experimentation. Since the one element that both vivisector and animal share in common is a capacity for suffering, the vivisector should in his own conscience refuse to inflict any pain that he would not himself be willing to undergo.

Thus one can accept the case which has been made by the medical profession for the use of animals in laboratory experiments provided that there is virtually no pain, even as one might justify the slaughter of animals for food, provided again that virtually no pain was inflicted — though one may be convinced that as human consciousness is intensified and as man not only is patient of evolution but guides and directs it, the barbarity of carnivorousness will be more and more realized. Before the fall, one may remember, there was no slaughtering of animals for food.

But that Roman Catholic theologians particularly, and Roman Catholic institutions defending vivisection, have tolerated the abuse of animals is doubly tragic because their theology, along with that of the whole Christian tradition, teaches that human suffering is not of itself an evil to be negated no matter what the cost. And this theology also teaches that human suffering finds full compensation in an afterlife which is theoretically denied to the suffering animal. Given these two assumptions, one would have thought the logical corollary to be that a *fortiori* it is sinful to cause needless pain in that aspect of creation which has — in the awesome phrase of Léon Bloy — "The air of trying to drown Cain in the calm lakes of its eyes."

I I

Catholics are growing more and more wary of the indiscriminate citation of papal statements to reinforce unstable doctrinal propositions. The circumspection extends not merely to ceremonial or occasional utterances of the popes but to encyclical letters of the past, and — though more questionably — even to recent encyclicals written about current topics and enjoined upon the faithful for their immediate acceptance. It requires, therefore, a great deal of temerity or naïveté for a moralist to invest some casual phrases of Pius XII with all the weight of "an official opinion of the Church" on the question of vivisection. Though there are certainly more crucial moral issues than vivisection facing mankind — nuclear war and the limitation of births being the most obvious — there is none which is more delicate, which requires more sensitivity for its adequate assessment, and which is more resistant to easy resolution by papal *obiter dicta*, above all *dicta* as imprecise, latinate and alien to the Anglo-American mind as the following:

There is nothing reproachable in simply killing an animal. . . . When there is good reason to slaughter and kill beasts, their cries should not arouse unreasonable compassion any more than do red-hot metals undergoing the blows of the hammer, seeds spoiling underground, branches crackling when they are pruned, grain that is surrendered to the harvester, wheat being ground by the milling machine.[8]

Since the Reformation, the loss of what Newman called the "English-German element in the Church" has engendered a monophysitism which dismisses not only humanity, but the "humanities" and the humanistic. It is not surprising, then, that

[8] Pius XII, quoted by James J. Quinn, S.J., "A Proper Respect for Men and Animals," *U. S. Catholic* (June, 1965).

it is only in the last few decades that Catholics have sought to formulate a theology of temporal realities, and that they have begun to concern themselves both with the material progress of man and with those movements properly called "humane." Nor is it surprising that every concrete expression of this concern has met with opposition from the defenders of social stasis and ecclesiastical angelism.

It is in the context of this relatively new discovery of the temporal that recent agitation by Catholics over animal experimentation must be placed. For we are faced here not with an accelerating sentimentalism, except perhaps among paranoids who attach themselves to all reform movements, but with another of many signs of the growing personalization of men and their works: a personalization that has always been retarded by theological and philosophical literalism and by specialized institutions which find in such literalism their moral and intellectual rationale. More specifically, and with regard to animal experimentation, it may be said that such personalization is impeded by the majority of Catholic moralists whose arguments bolster the vivisection stance of the A.M.A. — an organization as opposed to government regulation of laboratory experiments as to government regulation of national health services.

The crux of the moralists' argument is that because animals have no rights, man may treat them as he wishes so long as he does not thereby degrade himself. This argument evidently had more cogency in an age when such clearly defined categories as sadism or perversity covered the full range of cruelty. But in the age of "the button," in the age of an Eichmann, those categories have been shattered and with them the canons of conduct so confidently laid down by classical morality. We now know a refined cruelty, a calculated barbarism, which is the consequence of a network of causes, and which in its effects is so remote from its perpetrators, that even if a man is totally implicated in the eventual horror he is not manifestly degraded as a person. The parts of the machine are so elaborately interconnected that, though each of them is indispensable, no single one seems to bear the entire thrust of the evil act; thus self-recrimination and personal responsibility evaporate. A moral code which defines degradation to man as the outer limit of cruelty to animals is obsolete. There are laboratories in which the most severe pain is inflicted on animals in an atmosphere of such aseptic purity by teams of such well-educated, benign practitioners of medicine and psychology that the entire operation has about it the aura of philanthropy. In fact it is stained by what I can only regard as moral corruption.

Let us be precise about what is at issue. Again, there is no objection to animal experimentation as such — on condition that the infliction of severe pain be avoided as a grievous evil. The following dilemma will briefly summarize the grounds whereon this position stands or falls. Suppose that, through a suspension of the laws of physiology, someone lying on his deathbed could be cured by, say, the dismembering of a live cat. Would such an act be morally permissible? If this example is too remote, perhaps the dilemma may be made more precise in this way: can I, at this moment, pluck from their sockets the four limbs of a living animal in order to save my own life? To those who would answer with an unequivocal "yes," nothing more can be said; for them what follows will seem only rampant emotionalism.

If it is countered that vivisection never involves that kind of horror, one can only accept or dispute that as a fact. If it could never involve such horror, there is no issue, but if it has, one must acknowledge its monstrosity and even if it might in the future, one must demand justice. Now the fact is that vivisection has involved such horror in the past, that it still does, and that the medical profession is intent on its continuing to do so.

A complete catalog of these outrages stifles the spirit, but a few examples must be offered. At Columbia University anesthetized dogs received "700 to 1000 blows on each leg. As soon as the injury had been inflicted, the administration of ether was discontinued."[9] At Johns Hopkins pressure of "approximately 500 pounds" was applied to the thighs of anesthetized animals. The pressure was applied for five hours, but "no form of therapy was carried out after its removal."[10] At Tulane University and the University of Rochester 43 dogs were subjected to scalding burns covering approximately 70 percent of the body surface, inflicted by immersing them in water at a temperature fifteen

---

[9] The American Journal of Physiology (January, 1947).
[10] Surgery, Gynecology, and Obstetrics (October, 1942).

degrees below boiling with no post-experiment anesthesia.[11] At Harvard "pigs were laid on a grate about two feet over the pans" filled with flaming gasoline; "air temperatures as high as 900° C. were obtained for very brief periods."[12] At the Army Chemical Center, Maryland, "goats [were] tethered in slit trenches and subjected to fire bomb attack, which produced a fire ball of brief duration." "Animals received generalized burns from the fireball, or localized burns from spattering with gasoline." "34 percent of the animals on ground surface and two percent in the slit trenches were dead within ten minutes."[13]

In each case the experiments involve the inflicting of a degree of pain which can only be described as immoral — unless, of course, we regard the alleged end, the physical betterment of man, as justifying any and all means for its attainment, a moral doctrine apparently embraced by the author of the *U. S. Catholic* article previously cited, where he asserted that, "Surely the conquest of disease and the alleviation of suffering are grounds for some painful trials."

Even more atrocious are the experiments carried out to test reactions to what are called "noxious stimulations," that is, experiments in which the inflicting of severe pain is the immediate aim of the researcher. For example, at the University of Oregon cats were forced to walk on hot tiles and suffer pin pricks in their paws; this caused them "to leap into the air and frequently hit the top of the test apparatus. If they landed on the pins they would jerk their paws aside vigorously. . . . "[14] At Johns Hopkins after cats had been pinched, slapped, and spanked *by hand*, a researcher noted that this "elicited only a few plaintive meows." But when a cat's tail "was grasped between the jaws of a large surgical clamp . . . she cried loudly and attempted to escape." "During the 139 days of survival" this animal was subjected to increasing charges of electricity, the greatest of which "produced a third-degree burn. . . . "[15]

---

[11] *Surgical Forum* (No. 10, 1959).

[12] *Symposium on Burns*, National Research Council, 1950.

[13] *Ibid.*

[14] *Journal of Neurophysiology* (No. 21, 1958).

[15] *Proceedings of the Association for Research in Nervous and Mental Diseases* (No. 27, 1948).

Perhaps the most revolting of all experiments are those carried out by psychologists. In these experiments it is generally not a matter of research by medical doctors for the improvement of human health; more frequently the experiments are purely speculative undertakings carried out by graduate students in a discipline which competes with "'Education" for the lowest esteem of members of the academic community. Since these experiments differ mainly in purpose and not in method from those already discussed, there is no need to detail them here. Instead, I confine myself to quoting from a young researcher who, "in partial fulfillment of the requirements of the Ph.D. degree" at the University of Southern California, invented a completely light-free cage, the primary advantage of which "is that it permits the control of a rat's *lifetime* visual experience."[16] All of the literature which discusses such experiments is available, yet no American moral theologian has ever interrupted his litanies to Pius XII's "official opinion" to discuss the obvious "degradation to man" to which these documents attest.

To all suggestions by various humane organizations that government controls be imposed on researchers to avoid excessive pain, duplication and inadequate post-operative care (controls long accepted and praised by British scientists), Dr. Arthur Brayfield, Executive Director of the American Psychological Association replies: "Innovative research, particularly in the pilot-study stage, does not necessarily proceed according to a well-defined plan. It frequently has the characteristics of a multiple-contingency situation."[17] In the language of the layman, it is a fishing expedition where anything or nothing might turn up. Or, faced with the recommendation that limits be imposed on animal experimentation similar to those accepted by scientists in Denmark, England, Norway, Sweden and Switzerland — countries which have produced more Nobel laureates in medical research than the United States — American researchers are likely to agree with Dr. Bennet Cohen's testimony before the House Subcommittee on Health and Safety, in which he said: "I think

---

[16] *Journal of the Experimental Analysis of Behavior* (April, 1963).
[17] *Subcommittee Report on H.R. 1937, 87th Congress* (Washington, 1962), p. 269.

that the greatest sanction that can be provided against any scientist is the disapproval of his peers."[18]

Yet common sense says that scientists are no different from most other men, and common experience indicates that no profession has ever proved capable of policing itself. It has always required the control, or the indirect pressure, of the community as a whole to restrain the self-serving projects of particular groups. This is true of industry, labor unions, merchandising, agriculture, education, and every other sector of society. It is arrogance of the doctor-knows-best variety to assume it should not also apply to medicine. Moreover, such regulation would not only aid researchers by enforcing higher standards of care for the laboratory animal, it would also prevent their work from being unduly hampered by fanatic antivivisectionist groups opposed even to pain-free experiments. Nevertheless, the collective hubris of the American scientist has got so out of hand that no official body of researchers will discuss with representatives of humane societies a common basis for any legislation.

In the presence of a situation acknowledged as scandalous by religious and scientific authorities in other countries, what has been the response of American Catholic moralists? Faced by overwhelming, documented evidence of the abuse of animals, Catholic theologians have remained mute or repeated ad nauseam that "animals have no rights" — a proposition in itself questionable and in this instance irrelevant. Almost all of these moralists have explicated that proposition with a uniquely deracinated logic, laced with texts such as the one from Pius XII, cited earlier.

Almost invariably the Catholic moralist feels called upon to conclude his apology for all forms of vivisection with an appeal for conversion from a preoccupation with animal suffering to a concern for "people" — as if the two were mutually exclusive. "Anti-vivisectionists create the impression that they would rather see their children diseased than to see scientific experiments performed on poor little rats."[19] And in a statement defending bullfighting, Arthur O'Brien, C.S.C., wrote of its opponents: "They cry out that animals must have adequate housing, good food and medical facilities, while around them their fellowmen

---

[18] Ibid., p. 320.

[19] J. D. Conway, The Catholic Standard, September 9, 1963.

lack these same essentials and go unnoticed."[20] One might also "cry out" that it is precisely in those countries where the "artistic" torture of animals is sanctioned that the social improvement of people has been least evident — where, moreover, social justice has been impeded by the same theology of stasis which defends bullfighting.

Lastly, Archbishop Philip M. Hannan, in attacking proposed Congressional controls of medical experimentation, also mocked those concerned over the abuse of animals: " . . . any human being, no matter how poor and sick and fallen, no matter how insignificant and forgotten, is worth more than any number of the majestic wolfhounds Mrs. Irene Castle McLaughlin parades about the country in anti-vivisection demonstrations."[21] Such derisive nonsequiturs betray the fixed mentality of the special-pleader who will not or can not argue his case in the forum of rational debate. It is an elementary truism that in a complex world not everyone can pursue the general goals of humanity through the same channels. That some people are dedicated to the animal-welfare movement is no more surprising than that other people should be dedicated to, say, the construction of a national shrine in honor of the Immaculate Conception. Diversification is a law of progress.

The assumption of these clergymen that advocates of pain-free experiments would prefer to see people rather than animals suffer has been undermined by recent evidence — published mainly by animal-welfare groups — that more and more researchers, compelled by the drive for success in their own narrow specialty, are resorting to experiments on human beings. A British scientist has compiled a list of five hundred such experiments, and Dr. Henry K. Beecher of Harvard University in a study, "Ethics and the Explosion of Human Experimentation," has itemized twenty recent experiments on people — one of which, he notes, resulted in "25 men crippled, perhaps for life." Contrary to the insinuations of the moralists quoted above, it has been the members of various humane societies who have done most to draw attention to the heinousness of human experimentation.

[20] Albany *Times-Union*, February 16, 1963.
[21] *The Catholic Standard*, May 17, 1963.

Given the theological and philosophical weakness of the arguments put forward by clerical defenders of painful experimentation on animals, one can only be startled at being told repeatedly that the Hannan thesis represents the "official" view of the Church. The truth is that here, as with so many other "official" views, there can be no meaningful statement by Church authorities until the question is studied in depth, in the light of incontrovertible facts and of the new ranges of human sensibility which have been disclosed in the twentieth century. Until such study is undertaken there can be only provisional norms — norms which, in my opinion, are already obsolete. There is little point, therefore, in moralists' triumphantly asserting that the eminently sensible National Catholic Society for Animal Welfare has been "reprimanded by a Church official."[22] Church officials have been wrong before. And with regard to this particular official, it should be added that he also reprimanded the Fathers of Vatican II for their preliminary acceptance of the draft text on nuclear war, that he reprimanded the president of the Catholic Historical Association for his inaugural address criticizing McCarthyism, and that he reprimanded the Catholic press for its "un-Catholic" critical spirit. Such a plethora of "official" reprimands should not obscure the fact that no single bishop, not even the Metropolitan of New Orleans, speaks for the Church.

The melancholy conclusion must be that Catholic leadership has lagged, leaving this aspect of social morality to secular humanists and non-Catholics. And it is their arguments — not those of Catholic moralists — which will inevitably bring about the needed reform. Their basic argument, the one that will prove most persuasive to the electorate, is that if there is no abuse of animals, as the experimenters maintain, why oppose legislation that will simply codify this allegedly happy state of affairs? No decent parent has ever opposed laws aimed at punishing those who abuse children.

The failure of Catholic moralists to address themselves to the proven abuse of laboratory animals, while expatiating upon the unquestioned inferiority of animals to man, is comparable to the failure of just-war theorists to address themselves to the existence

---

[22] Quinn, *loc. cit.*

of an overkill capacity, and of social moralists to address themselves to the existence of de facto segregation. Neither the animals-
have-no-rights assumption, nor the just-war theory, nor the
brothers-of-Christ doctrine has any relevance to anyone — except
to Catholic theologians of Laputa — unless it plunges its roots
into the existential, unless it confronts and transforms the world
of the here and now.

XI

THE FUTURE OF
BELIEF DEBATE

Forty years ago when Karl Rahner was a student, the writings
of one of his confreres of the preceding generation, Joseph
Maréchal, were scorned and proscribed in almost all Catholic
seminaries, particularly those of the Jesuits. Rahner, who was
forced to read Maréchal secretly after hours when his fellow-
seminarians as well as his superiors were asleep, has referred to
himself as "the Nicodemus of Maréchal," that is, as one who,
like Nicodemus in the gospel, came to know the truth "by
night," who derived the basic insight animating all his subsequent works from these nocturnal forays into Maréchal's famous
fifth cahier where Kant is put into the service of Aquinas. Now
Maréchallian Thomism, where there is any functionally relevant
Thomism at all, holds the field, and a new philosophy, which
according to its critics puts all things in doubt, is the current
candidate for condemnation and censure, and unquestionably
somewhere is being conned by flashlight in seminary garret or
basement by the Nicodemuses of a new generation. With the
usual ironies of history, the most effective assaults upon this
new object of banning and burning — Leslie Dewart's *The Future
of Belief*[1] — are coming from the same Maréchallian Thomism
which four decades ago was itself the butt of the interdicts
of officialdom.

However, we have more to do with here than merely a matter
of current philosophical vogues. For the author of *The Future
of Belief* is not simply challenging a rival school of thought,
he is calling into question a whole tradition's way of grappling

[1] New York, 1966.

with the concept of God. This is a revolutionary enterprise, and Dewart is both philosophically and politically conscious of his revolutionary heritage. Born in Spain during a decade of bloody anti-monarchist uprisings, a bomber pilot on submarine patrol in World War II, and an ardent defender in the world press of the Castro rebellion against Batista, Dewart does not view the dislocation engendered by radical changes, whether religious or social, as a necessary evil.

But the revolutionary label may be misleading for Dewart would contend that his is not some kind of subversive mission aimed at overthrowing the beliefs of modern Christians. On the contrary, he suggests, those beliefs have already been bankrupted by the pressures and forces released in the last century of intellectual history, by the new insights born of Marx, Darwin, and Freud, and represented in orthodox Christianity by the achievement of Teilhard. The real subversives, then, would be those fundamentalists — Blondel's "veterists" — who in the name of an ossified tradition refuse to recognize this bankruptcy and continue to preach a God and a church that have no bearing on twentieth-century man. Unfortunately, as soon as one says "twentieth-century man" a formidable problem arises, because both veterists and modernists, conservatives and liberals, contend they have nothing else but his good at heart, and that they alone know best what his real feelings and needs are.

Thus the initial premise, on which everything subsequent hinges, borders on the sociological: who truly speaks for that "contemporary experience" on which both Dewart and his severest qualified critics — Michael Novak, David Burrell, H. de Lavalette: Maréchallians all — peg their antagonist views.[2] Michael Novak, in a needlessly shrill *Commonweal* review, insisted relentlessly that Dewart simply was not familiar with the secular mind of today, that he was merely a kind of academic bystander. And combining high dudgeon with low blows, Novak went on to oblate his own personal anguish over napalm bombs, bloodshed in Cicero, etc., as evidence of his own superior qualifications as trustee and legatee of the common man's "contemporary experience." Whom one ought to believe probably won't be known

---

[2] *Commonweal* (February 3, 1967); *The New Scholasticism* (Summer, 1967); *Continuum* (Spring, 1967).

until the sociologists speak up; but on a priori grounds — and notwithstanding the introduction of shudders over war and racism — there is no more reason for thinking that Mr. Novak, only a few years out of seminary and graduate school, has any tighter a grasp on the hard realities of secularity than does Dr. Dewart who in his late teens fled alone from tyranny in Cuba, flew with the RAF, charted the rationale of the Castro revolution, and has agitated repeatedly for U. S. disengagement in Vietnam: the latter during a period, one is embarrassed to recall, when Mr. Novak with neo-Niebuhrian punctilio was defending the American role in that mad conflict. If the discernment of the signs of the time requires some empathy with the spirit of the times, one imagines that Dewart's credentials are at least as much to be honored as those of any of his critics who have thus far spoken up. But of course, ultimately if one is going to judge which of the two opposing views is the more accurate he will just have to look carefully at both of them and see which of the two better jibes with his own "contemporary experience."

One thing is certain. Dewart seems to have exposed the distortions that are latent in the beliefs of great numbers of restless Christians. Nothing else can explain the extraordinary impact of his book which is at once abstruse, obscure, here rigorously argued and there lyrically elliptic, highly sophisticated throughout, fascinating in what it offers and infuriating in what it portends but does not explicitate. For a book as difficult as Dewart's to enjoy such immediate fame and to be so quickly translated into other tongues (French, German, Spanish, Catalan, Portuguese, and Polish translations are in preparation) one cannot invoke the conventional public-relations formulas in explanation — though the phenomenal acclaim for the book has been ascribed to the fact that (1) Roman Catholics are awed by celebrated Protestant thinkers, (2) Harvey Cox, celebrated . . . etc., has praised Dewart's work in glowing terms, (3) therefore: instant popularity. The reason Cox liked the book, it is further alleged, is that Protestants will applaud any attack on Scholasticism. But the truth is, as every publisher and every author knows, no endorsements from however high up can galvanize a book into a vitality it doesn't natively possess. As for Cox's praise, it was based explicitly on

Dewart's "doctrine of God," and not on any anti-Scholastic leanings. Moreover, it is growing clearer day after day that the attractiveness of Dewart's premises, if not of his entire program, to such distinguished non-Catholics as the Calvinist Vahanian, the Baptist Cox, the Anglican Macquarrie, and the Marxist Garaudy is due to the realization that all institutionalized dogmatisms are trammeled by the same or similar cultural growths as those encrusting Roman Catholicism. The ecumenical import of Dewart's work is the result of its addressing itself to the common problems of atheists and believers, Catholics and non-Catholics. The demand for answers to such problems is very deeply and very widely felt.

The Dewart project, then, is not just some spasmodic reaction within the Catholic camp to such extramural fads as secularization or the death of God; though both of those, even when marketed by the media like hoola hoops and miniskirts, have been important in articulating the two central themes in modern religious culture: the act-centeredness, that is, the radical historicity of religion, and the cleavage between real belief and official theologies. ("God is dead" was really a Protestant rune for "theology as traditionally undertaken is dead.") Dewart's book, as an embodiment of these two themes, is utterly open to history, and therefore is in the best sense of the word, Teilhardian.

That is why "dehellenization" looms so large in his program — though that is not the aptest description of what Dewart wants. The word is too negative, like the English "demythologize"; what is needed is a more affirmative concept, like "Entmythologisierung," a concept that might then be translated "the personalizing of history." As everyone knows, for sixty years or so biblical students have been pointing up the disparity between the scriptural understanding of man and the notion of man embodied in what may loosely be termed the hellenic tradition. All that, as Michael Novak has correctly noted, is a commonplace. It is also *not* what Dewart is primarily concerned about. His preoccupation is with the more fundamental fact that because the hellenic understanding of man negated his reality as a being in history, there was no possibility of relating the experience of self-consciously evolutionary man, of modern man, to a religious doctrine inextricably bound to ahistorical categories. All churchmen could offer, up till now, was the option of bending the will, that is, of distorting lived experience, in order to conform it to a static conception of reality.

Dewart would be the last to suggest that the hellenization of Christianity has been simply catastrophic; rather what he is objecting to is the perpetuation of the hellenic mindset in an evolutionary age, in an age of technology, in an age when man is knowingly shaping his own culture. The hellenization of dogma could hardly be regarded as an unmixed evil: Dewart is very explicit on that point. Hellenization was an imperative in its own time; it was the necessary response of churchmen in a given age to their own history. But blind fidelity to this legacy now would be to live an institutionalized lie, for in the present age history demands a different response.

But an adequate response is not merely inhibited by the fact that one cultural pattern from the past is stifling the emerging pattern of the present; even more, it is inhibited by the fact that it is intrinsic to that earlier pattern that the very possibility of any other cultural pattern be denied. Those who would argue against dehellenization as implying a rupture in the continuity of mankind's spiritual achievement fail to recognize that the hellenic Denkform (i.e., mindset) is by definition inimical to the only continuity modern man knows: the continuity of discontinuity. As Bernard Lonergan has noted in "Dimensions of Meaning," "Classical culture cannot be jettisoned without being replaced; and what replaces it, cannot but run counter to classical expectations."[3]

The traditional identification of God as "being," as supreme Being, is regarded by Dewart as typical of the hellenic hang-up. Once God is so denominated, it is suggested, there is no way that he can be immanent to man and his history except by a quasi-pantheist confusion with whatever else that is: in fact, nothing else truly is. If Being is being, God is creation. To avoid such patent heresy, as Dewart sees it, Catholicism has tended to pay lip service to an immanent God while in practice worshiping one who was entirely and only transcendent. It is true

---

[3] *Collection* (New York, 1967), p. 266.

that both traditional philosophy and theology have a devisal
for apparently obviating Dewart's difficulty: the theologians call
it the distinction between created and uncreated grace, and the
philosophers call it the analogy of being. In either case one
is faced with the construction of a tautology to explain the
radical paradox of a God at once immanent and transcendent.
Dewart would not fault the tradition at that point: all speculative thought is ultimately the tautologizing of paradox. His
criticism would be that the analogical character of the being-
Being polarity is true neither to God's immanence nor to his
transcendence, and that it is therefore equally untrue to man's
historicity and his destiny. In the practical order, as a result
of the failure of Christianity to maintain a hold on one of the
poles of the paradox (the divine immanence), not merely was
God conceived to be *really* only "out there," but the Christian's
existence in history was effectively undercut, his commitment
to the temporal order, to "this world," was dissolved in favor
of his service of the "other world" where his God *really* dwelt.
The task of building the earth was seen as a mere sideline,
when it was not entirely condemned — as by nineteenth-century
Catholicism — as "anthropocentric humanism."

For speculative and practical reasons, therefore, Dewart would
wish to conceive God as something other than "being," even
though it is only *in* being that we discover a reality that is
beyond being. This reality "beyond being" is the God that
Dewart is somehow seeking to limn. For Dewart there is no
opposition between God's immanence and his transcendence because it is God's experienced presence in being that leads man
beyond being. As he remarked in his *Commonweal* "God" paper:
"The transcendence of the genuinely immanent God means
this: if the God whom we find always here is not to vanish into
thin air, if he is not to become an idol, if he is not to be
reduced to the totality of being, and if he is not to be explained
away as the becoming of the world or the projection of man —
in a word, if the God who is actually *here* within being is the
God of Christian tradition, it follows that he is not to be
conceived as being."[4]

---

[4] February 10, 1967.

In sum there are two reasons for abandoning the concept of God as subsistent Being: the first — which sociologists will have to debate — is that it does not answer to the spiritual longings of contemporary man; the second — which historically would seem not to be debatable, though difficult of explicitation theoretically — is that it effectively negates God's immanence, and in practice leads to the traditional "Christian" attitudes of contempt for the world, disdain for the concrete and the temporal. The positive explicitation of what is thus far in Dewart a negative critique will therefore be crucial to the success of his project, and must necessarily be the theme of his future work. If God is not to be conceived as being, yet somehow must be "conceptualized," how is he to be conceived? What would seem to be called for immediately is a phenomenology of presence which will ultimately sketch out what the something *is* that is present.

This writer is convinced that in pursuit of that goal Dewart will enrich our understanding of the God-concept immeasurably; this writer is less convinced that Dewart may not end up, if not a Maréchallian Thomist, then a kind of Maréchallian existentialist. The Blondel-Maréchal-late-Lonergan axis would seem then to be strengthened rather than cracked by the following from the Introduction to the forthcoming French edition of *The Future of Belief*:

Yet, this view need not imply that faith (that is, religious experience) is *reducible* to non-religious, secular or "natural" experience. Quite the contrary, the point is that *ordinary* human experience is *insufficient* unless it extends itself into a new extra-ordinary dimension. When it so extends itself, experience becomes *religious* experience or faith. Thus, the apparent opposition between faith and experience simply means this: precisely insofar as experience is *immanent* to the being of man, experience has a *transcendent* dimension, namely faith. But faith *transcends* experience only because faith is the transcendence *of experience*. Faith does not transcend experience by *ceasing* to be experience. Faith is, as it were, the *ultimate* meaning of that which *already* exists, namely, human experience.

Furthermore, with regard to the future of *The Future of Belief*, Dewart would probably say that the goal of reconceptualization cannot be realized here and now — and of course never realized fully: that just as the notion of God as subsistent being repre-

sented the climax of centuries of speculation which were nurtured as much by non-Christian insights as by biblical data, so
too the formulation of the non-hellenic concept of God is yet
to come. But as Teilhard would say it is as much *en avant* as
en haut: the two in fact are converging.

If one truly believes in salvation history (and that is the key
to Dewart's doctrine) then the reconceptualization will be the
product of another marriage of biblical revelation with philosophical insights that are not formally Christian. But one should not
overemphasize "philosophical" insights since it is a question, in
moving toward more significant formulae of belief, of travelling
a *via practica*. The meaning of the experience of God's presence
to men in this world will be elaborated through the interplay
of a host of historical and social factors (including necessarily
those of the past that can survive) with a correlative new and
deeper understanding of the gospels and of the mission of the
Church. Since we are talking about a truly existential understanding of man, about an understanding which is empirically
based and socially committed, one would expect to see all the
resources of all the humane sciences drawn upon, and most particularly those which are specifically concerned with the personal
and concrete, that is with the "esthetic." Purely by way of
casual examples from the present of the kinds of insights this
radically future-oriented religious philosophy will have to depend
upon, one might think of those flowing from Hugo Rahner's
theology of play and dance,[5] from Joseph Powers' use of communication theory in a theology of the Real Presence,[6] from
William Lynch's grasp of the function of the dramatic for a,
perhaps unformulated, theology of death;[7] and hopefully, somewhere in that future Dewart is tentatively charting, a yet unborn
thinker may construct a theology on Rilke's aphorism, *Gesang
ist Dasein*.

The watchword of the entire program will be the recently
coined phrase, "*doing* philosophy." "Speculation," "theorizing"
— etymology notwithstanding — can no longer mean as they did
for the ancients and for the scholastics a mere "seeing," any more

---

[5] *Man at Play* (New York, 1966).
[6] *Eucharistic Theology* (New York, 1967).
[7] Cf. "Death as Nothingness," *Continuum* (Autumn, 1967).

than faith can be conceived as merely intellectual assent, or the bliss of the blessed as a beatific vision. The phrase, "to do" philosophy or theology is, first, more nearly true to the experience of our encounter with the world and others as entailing not so much a looking at as an action and transaction; and second, is closely akin to the injunction of St. Paul that we should "do the truth." It is this act-centered, historical dimension that is at the bottom of Dewart's dehellenization project and also of his solution to the dilemma that, on the one hand, "although we do not experience God he must be nonetheless Being," and on the other, "that we do experience God, although evidently we do not experience him as being."

Without entirely endorsing either of those propositions, one must still maintain, as does the present writer, that Dewart has undeniably addressed himself to a major aspect, if not the major aspect, of the malaise of that contemporary man who is, in Pascal's words, "wounded by mystery." And one would hope that rather than the acrimonious and cavilling criticism to which his work has too often thus far been subjected, thinkers of differing religious and philosophical perspectives might try to grapple with the issues on his terms, even as he has so obviously grappled with them on theirs. It is no contribution whatever to decry his entire effort on the grounds that the brand of scholasticism he is indicting is not quite as pure as some others he allegedly skirted because they were less vulnerable. The fundamental presupposition of Dewart and of his writings has been that we must take our point of departure from present existent realities; and while the scholasticism he is opposing may not be, in this or that partisan's view, the most orthodox or creative or rigorous or up-to-date, it is undeniably the most influential on historical Christian belief. That Maréchal may be a more formidable Thomist than Maritain — who is to say? — is largely irrelevant. Maréchal has been a considerably less influential Thomist than Maritain, and most emphatically so in the English-speaking world for which Dewart is writing.

What one would prefer to the present lamentations on the part of Maréchallian Thomists that Dewart has ignored them would be an effort to engage him in close debate on specific topics. Obviously neither Dewart nor any brand of Thomist can afford to simply affirm that experience implies this or that. Any such affirmation must be correlated with large areas of history and sociology, must be supported by analogous evidence from individual psychology and political life, and must be integrated with other broad-gauge theories of scientific and philosophic understanding. Thus far it is clear that Dewart has bolstered his general contention — God cannot now be conceived as subsistent being — by a brilliant critique of Gilson's epistemology, by a global synthesis of some prevalent currents in non-scholastic religious philosophy (notably Tillich and Marcel), by an assessment of the phenomenon of Marxist socialism and of the unifying of humanity. The convergence of all these elements on one focus makes his a very strong point, and if it is going to be blunted his critics will have to answer him patiently, not denounce him shrilly. One of Dewart's own favorite quotes is from Heidegger: "Zealous attempts at refutation never get us on a thinker's path."

It is true Dewart himself has not always appeared to make his critic's task an easy one. He has not, of course, demeaned his cause by descending to personal polemic with some of his opponents who have brashly called into question his academic competence, his moral judgment, his mere understanding of the world. But he has left himself a kind of moving target — which, however, is exactly what one would expect of a consistent "projective" and non-retrospective philosopher. The book, after all, is called The FUTURE of Belief. Nor is this a particularly novel style of religious speculation in our time: it is characteristic of Schillebeeckx's unfinished sacramental theory, of Rahner's "investigations," and von Balthasar's "sketches." That it is the only possible style or the best possible style in an age of transition, the existence of so masterly a work as Lonergan's Insight would seem to deny. But it is without question a style which has been sanctioned by the creative thought it has generated.

What the controversy over Dewart's book fines itself down to, then, is not certainly an academic debate over the real distinction of essence and existence (a highly serviceable formula), nor even over the more weighty question of how we denominate "God" — more weighty because even the cleanest ascriptions, once fabricated, crystallize our thinking. What the debate is really over is the very nature of man's understanding of his world. For Dewart, history is not just the setting, is not just the background, is not just the framework of man's knowledge; it is the very "principle" that "structures" it. There can be therefore no eternal verities, or at least no eternal verities understandable as such. The only absolute truth discernible is that there is no absolute truth discernible. This is frightening: one had not known the wound in nature went so deep. It is frightening, and precisely because it is, salvation is revealed through this very wound, in history. As corollary, there can be no universal synthesis of knowledge, but only variant clusters coherent within themselves and, hopefully, not too at odds with one another taken individually. The Age of Aquinas and Spinoza is over; dead as well is *The Degrees of Knowledge* and even *The Unity of Philosophical Experience*. This, with all it implies, is what is at issue.

One should hardly be surprised that the severest responsible criticism of Dewart has been made by the disciples of the most challenging and stimulating systematic thinker within the Christian community, Bernard Lonergan. On both sides of the division is intelligence and sophistication, complete fidelity to the living Church and total commitment to the Christian message. On the one hand is continuity, order, and incredible breadth of learning; on the other is radical penetration into the concrete, the empiric, and profound insight into the actuality of the immediate present. *The Future of Belief* is the testing ground on which will be determined what accommodations can be tolerated by the two different approaches without destroying the essential orientation of either. A genuinely eirenic spirit will be required of the participants on both sides. But this is hardly unattainable, both because we have reached a stage in philosophical discussion where a healthy strain of ambiguity necessarily emerges, and because there remain, notwithstanding many differences, intersecting vectors marking off a large patrimony which both viewpoints must share. Apart from a common reliance on revelation there is the kind of mutually acceptable ground which the following from Dewart exemplifies:

Every man sooner or later in his life confronts himself as a being, grasps the awful reality of the fact that he really exists. When we so meet existence, I think we come in contact with a reality which points to something beyond all that it itself is — despite the fact that it itself is *all* that we experience.[8]

Of course, no one would imply that the differences will be resolved merely by translating from one idiom to another; but it is obvious that at least there is enough by way of shared premises for genuine dialogue to begin.

I close with some words from Lonergan on the transitional period from a classical to a nonclassical culture:

There is bound to be formed a solid right that is determined to live in a world that no longer exists. There is bound to be formed a scattered left, captivated by now this, now that new development, exploring now this and now that new possibility. But what will count is a perhaps not numerous center, big enough to be at home in both the old and the new, painstaking enough to work out one by one the transitions to be made, strong enough to refuse half-measures and insist on complete solutions even though it has to wait.[9]

But a center can only exist in terms of its boundaries, one component of which is by definition that left which *The Future of Belief* now holds.

---

[8] Preface, *loc. cit.*
[9] Lonergan, *loc. cit.*, p. 267.

XII

DICTION AS MORALITY

Diction is morality in the immediate sense that language requires what grammarians call "word order"; it requires that the outburst of feeling and emotion be controlled and restrained if it is to be made communicable. Mere passion and emotion are the chaos out of which order is wrought by being worded. But the submission of feeling to word order like the submission of man to the natural order is no more abjection before some absolute datum, before some unchanging rule, than conformity to a grammatical paradigm is speech. The question, "How do I know what I mean until I say it?" on the moral plane signifies that it is only in the very act of doing something that we discover right and wrong.

These are largely commonplaces which illustrate not so much that diction is morality as that language-acts parallel ethical acts. But this is not what is of primary concern here. If morality is what man does to attain his proper destiny (whatever that may be), then moral acts are acts that make for happiness. And conversely anything which engenders happiness entails an exercise of morality.[1] But even this is still too global and cerebral: it requires finer articulation and an empiric base if it is to be made cogent.

What I want to do is look at certain framings of language

---

[1] "Every creature who fulfills itself in joy does the will of God." Theodore Haecker, *Journal in the Night* (New York, 1950), p. 220. The working hypothesis is that man's destiny is *Daseinsfreude*; that *Gesang ist Dasein* (*Sonette an Orpheus*, I, iii); therefore pleasing diction is good morality. *"Je dis que le coeur aime l'être universel naturellement . . . "* (*Pensées et Opuscules*, Brunschvicg ed., p. 458). To keep notes to a minimum only pivotal texts will be identified.

that by common consent make man happy, and seek to discern precisely and specifically how and why these are exercises in morality. The emphasis is on the framing of language not on its statements, on the patterning of words, not on their lexical content — recognizing the while that with all verbal sequences it is not possible to say that what they signify can be separated entirely from the way they are organized. But it is the pattern, not the paraphraseable meaning, that interests us. Since pattern-centered speech is poetry and meaning-centered speech is prose, it is poetic texts that must be scrutinized.

We are in search of standards, but even more, of the reason why certain lines of poetry are standards. As every undergraduate has been told, Arnold's touchstones were touchstones primarily of a literal meaning with which Arnold was sympathetic because it conveyed something of his own ethical outlook: an outlook that was intrinsically disoriented by the very fact that pattern-speech was being subverted to content-speech ends: "E'n la sua volontade è nostra pace" (approved by Eliot also, one suspects, on Arnoldian grounds); "And courage never to submit or yield / And what is else not to be overcome"; and, "which cost Ceres all that pain / To seek her through the world" (the latter an important fragment, but sanctioned here only for its evocation of chin-up conduct). So, too, with the negative touchstones Arnold supplied for prose in "The Literary Influence of Academies." The prose he lauds as "prose of the centre," "prose without the note of provinciality," is contrasted with four passages from Burke redolent of oral-anal imagery all highly offensive to mid-Victorian moral sensibilities. But in the touchstones we have to do with, the patent moral content is negligible, and for that reason among others, the statements are all the more profoundly ethical and therefore all the more profoundly satisfying.

We may approach the issue from two directions. We may begin with a conception of man, and see if this conception is somehow ratified in the patterning of certain unquestionably pleasing lines. Since somehow man and poetry are isomorphic — otherwise poetry wouldn't be pleasing at all — we will not be surprised if man defined by philosophers as *Geist in Welt*, *esprit incarné*, existence-essence, universal-concrete, is congruous with poetry defined by Carlyle as the "infinite with the finite," or by Browning as the "infinite within the finite."[2] The terms are all analogous one with the other as each is only the tautology of some common undefinable paradox. Whether among German Romantic philosophers and their heirs or among English Romantic poets and their heirs, the definitions merge so that man and poetry are the felt-thought, the thought-feeling, the intellectualized-sensation, the irony of contingent over against absolute, the tension of extension and intention, etc. And any statement communicating this relation by its pattern will be truly poetic, truly human, and therefore truly moral. Being aware of all that, one's first mode of approach would be to take up unknown lines of verse and determine whether they somehow embody this relation; those that do, good; those that don't, bad. But this would be like constructing an ethical theory without ever having performed an ethical act; and since ontologically "feeling is first,"[3] (or as moralists say, conscience takes primacy) like all apriorisms, this approach leads only back to Arnold and the influence of academies (or among moralists, to scholasticism). The other mode would be to take avowedly admirable texts — on the undeniable premise that they are such precisely because of their connaturality with man — and see how they say something of human nature. At best the philosophers' assumptions are heuristic devisings which can only be verified by the poems. We begin, therefore, with poems.

A start can be made with that passage Arnold, for the wrong reasons, applauded: " . . . which caused Ceres all that pain to seek her through the world." This is a fragment, and by definition fragments find meaning only in relation to an unfragmented whole. We are not experiencing here merely another overtone of the eternal note of sadness, though that is what the statement

---

[2] *Sartor Resartus*, III, iii; *The Works of John Ruskin* (London, 1909), XXXVI, xxxiv.

[3] Cummings:

> since feeling is first
> who pays any attention
> to the syntax of things
> will never wholly kiss you.

The moral dilemma plays on the sin-tax and the holy kiss.

is all about. The complete passage, which on better grounds was one of Aldous Huxley's touchstones too, is:

> Not that fair field
> Of Enna, where Proserpin gath'ring flow'rs
> Herself a fairer Flow'r by gloomy Dis
> Was gather'd, which cost Ceres all that pain
> To seek her through the world . . .[4]

What we have here is not only a juxtaposition of flowers and pain, a common enough theme (reminiscent of Sassoon's "earth's nullity made strange by flowers"), not only a chiastic structure (gathering flowers / flower gathered) reminiscent of Stevens' "vital, fatal X," not only a collision of mellifluous polysyllables with stark monosyllables (reminiscent of all philosophers' vexation at the one-many problem) — though of course we do have all of this. But we are seeking the basic pattern, are in search of the shape of Stevens' "central poem" of which all these paradoxic structures are only the multiple reflection.[5] That central poem disclosed by its lesser mimes is the *relation* of limned foreground to unlimited background, the relation of individual, concrete, particular, single, temporal, to universal, absolute, eternal, etc. (cognates can be supplied ad libitum). When we experience that relation we are placed in our proper stance — hence, delight. We are made to know what we are, that is, we are being moral.

Let us take now a simpler illustration with a view to a more complicated exegesis, the induction to Lionel Johnson's "By the Statue of King Charles at Charing Cross" — the title itself suggests its own parallels with the Milton text: the splendid, the wounded, the chiastic:

> Somber and rich, the skies
> Great glooms, and starry plains;

---

[4] *Paradise Lost*, IV, pp. 268–272.
[5] Stevens, "A Primitive Like an Orb," VII:

> The central poem is the poem of the whole,
> The poem of the composition of the whole,
> The composition of blue sea and of green,
> Of blue light and of green, as lesser poems,
> And the miraculous multiplex of lesser poems,
> Not merely into a whole, but a poem of
> The whole, the essential compact of the parts,
> The roundness that pulls tight the final ring.

> Gently the night wind sighs;
> Else a vast silence reigns.
>
> The splendid silence clings
> Around me: and around
> the saddest of all Kings,
> Crown'd, and again discrown'd.

Thus is tragedy defined (and with slight adjustments, comedy as well). Against the immense screen of the seemingly indifferent absolute is projected the figure not of a fallen man, but of a man, in Aristotle's terms, fallen from the highest estate. Yet it is not even the figure of a man, but of something utterly more frangible; it is a mere effigy, a statue. This is Caesar dead and turned to clay, not to keep the wind away, but to signify the encompassment of all contingencies by what our forebears called the "sky-God" and what Johnson's contemporary, George William Russell, called "the great breath."[6] It is this relation that these lines evoke.

What says the Lord: "I have crowned you with honor and glory." But this beloved of Jehovah, as deutero-Isaiah foresees him suffering the great cosmic tragedy, becomes "a worm and no man." It is tragic that worm vainly aspire to kingship, that king vainly aspire to "absolute power" and "divine right." But it is also comic with an ambiguity disclosed by the friendly rejoinder, "I'll crown you if you do that again." The king crowned and again discrowned is just as tragic and just as comic as is the vaudeville banker, silk hat dislodged by a snowball, or the clown's pratfall. This kinship of comedy and tragedy accounts for the durable pairing in our literature of "emperor and clown," of Prince Hal and Falstaff, or the fusion of both in "the emperor of ice cream." The difference is only that in tragedy it is the absolute that seems to crush the contingent precisely because of the contingent's aspiration to the absolute: the tragic hero knows what he wants. Whereas in comedy the contingent is trapped in contingencies, and is defeated by them: that is

---

[6] I saw how all the trembling ages past,
Molded to her by deep and deeper breath,
Near'd to the hour when Beauty breathes her last
And knows herself in death.

funny because if man is only a little less than the angels, no little devils ought to be able to upset him.[7]

I don't mean to be precious. It is only when the contingent experiences the passion for the absolute that the tragic occurs; only when man experiences this relationship which is constituted by his own duality can there be tragedy. There is but one step from tragedy to comedy; it is the step from duality to triviality. Comedy, therefore, takes place only where multiplicity smothers man's vocation to unity, and where, as a consequence, nothing has any importance because nothing has any real meaning. Comedy is beyond morality. (In a monadic world there is no meaning and no morality because meaning and morality always demand a comparison, a duality, a relationship with something "other." And hence the grossly comic is described as "a panic.") This is why the relationship that Johnson's lines convey is tragic: the overarching *Umwelt* and the limned individual.

Even what we suspect on many other grounds is probably bad verse tends to move us by imposing on us this essentially human, and therefore essentially moral and tragic posture, as when almost unwillingly one responds to Browning's:

> Where the quiet-colored end of evening smiles
>   Miles and miles
> On the solitary pastures where our sheep
>   Half asleep. . . .[8]

And this is also why, for all their mournful rhetoric, there is no tragic accent in the following from *In Memoriam* — anodynes Lionel Johnson might almost have been hurling back at their prescriber:[9]

> And lest I stiffen into stone,
> I will not eat my heart alone,

---

[7] The devils stand in our tradition as the mediating representatives of utter contingency, even as the angels are the mediating representatives of the absolute. It is typical of the present era of prosey literalism in Roman Catholicism that while the most advanced of the avant-garde (cf. the new Dutch catechism) question the existence of evil and good spirits, the rest of the world should be forcibly reminded of their existence by a non-believer like Iris Murdoch in her *The Time of the Angels* — even as a reading of Rilke or Stevens would undercut that same avant-garde's denigration of the virgin birth of Jesus.

[8] "Love Among the Ruins."   [9] No. 108.

> Nor feed with sigh a passing wind;
> What profit lies in barren faith,
> And vacant yearning, though with might
> To scale the heaven's highest height,
> Or dive below the wells of death.

The archetypal *roi dépossédé* for English letters, whose perfect circular creation was broken at his fall, is Arthur whose pasch is described (very well, because this is early Tennyson):

> So all day long the noise of battle rolled
> Among the mountains by the winter sea,
> Until King Arthur's table, man by man,
> Had fallen in Lyonnesse about their lord
> King Arthur; then, because his wound was deep,
> The bold Sir Bedivere uplifted him. . . .[10]

" . . . because his wound was deep"; how casually interjected, and how ineffectually colliding with the vast horizon that forms the backdrop of the great king's maiming. The structural similarities to the other texts above are clear enough even to the concluding staccato spondees (as in "to seek her through the world"). Equally clear is the movement of the passage from *ces éspaces infinis* to man *blessé par le mystère*. But we have a new change rung on that *et ego in Arcadia* theme that Panofsky so brilliantly explicated and so understandably recurrent in our literature[11] — as in the only memorable lines of "Manfred":

> . . . upon such a night
> I stood within the Coliseum's wall,
> 'Midst the chief relics of almighty Rome;
> The trees which grew along the broken arches
> Waved dark in the blue midnight, and the stars
> Shone through the rents of ruin; from afar
> The watch-dog bayed beyond the Tiber; and
> More near from out the Caesar's palace came
> The owl's long cry. . . .[12]

We have more than this, however fine it is, in Tennyson's life-death, near-far cluster. The very casualty of the tragedy of Arthur

---

[10] For Pascal, man as such suffers the *misères d'un roi dépossédé* (p. 509); "Morte d'Arthur," 1–6.

[11] The essay is too important to go without citation. "Poussin and the Elegiac Tradition," in *Meaning in the Visual Arts* (New York, 1955).

[12] Act III, Scene iv.

is startling. "Then, because his wound was deep," is almost a parenthetic ejaculation, almost only a slight interruption breaking momently the flow of the whole period. It would seem that man, so seemingly promethean, is simply a mere afterthought in the forward flowing tide of things. Man is only a sob or sigh of the great breath, only as Donne says an aria in the musique of God — for which Wordsworth's solitary reaper is a less theologically geared symbol. Hence the gasp, the poignancy of such parenthetic utterances as:

> Or bid the soul of Orpheus sing
> Such notes as, *warbled to the string*,
> Drew iron tears down Pluto's cheek
> And made Hell grant what Love did seek.[13]

or again (another solitary reaper):

> Perhaps the self-same song that found a path
>   Through the sad heart of Ruth, when, *sick for home*,
> She stood in tears amid the alien corn.[14]

or, inversely:

> *Old Eben Flood*, climbing alone one night
> Over the hill between the town below
> And the forsaken upland hermitage
> That held as much as he should ever know
> On earth again of home, *paused warily*.[15]

In the last instance we return to our earlier figure of that wounded chief whom both Ruth and the sad virgin are only pale counterparts of; for Eben is also Roland at Roncevaux ("like Roland's ghost"),[16] Arthur in Lyonnesse, even as all likenesses of broken kings are only analogues of the central poem of the infinite engulfing and giving meaning to the definite.

As we have noted, the movement of the verse is from the great glooms and plains of the universal reaches to the slight

---

[13] "Il Penseroso," 105–108.
[14] "Ode to a Nightingale," 65-67
[15] "Mr. Flood's Party," 1–5.
[16] Alone as if enduring to the end
   A valiant armor of scarred hopes outworn,
   He stood there in the middle of the road,
   Like Roland's ghost winding a silent horn.

bent figure of the isolate individual. Within this infinite frame
the damaged image of finitude is trapped. This is tragedy of
the kind Bossuet essayed in prose in that memorable sermon on
the death of the great queen which moved through long stately
periods, then through shorter clauses to the pithy fulcrum pro-
claiming: the queen is dead.[17] The format is that of the ever-
widening gyre, at the foot of which stands the helpless falconer.[18]
But if, as Donne affirmed, "death doth touch the Resurrection,"[19] the *carmen figuratum* that Bossuet was homiletically
drawing is not merely that of the triangle on its tip (the terrifying
whirlpool of Phlebas the Phoenician):

It is something more: it is the "Easter Wings" of George Herbert
in which the tragic structure, set forth in each of the passages
we have cited, moving from infinite to finite, is complemented by
a *reditus* from that finite to the infinite:

> Lord, who createdst man in wealth and store,
>   Though foolishly he lost the same
>   Decaying more and more
>   Till he became
>   Most poore:

---

[17] "Oraison Funèbre de Henriette-Marie de France, Reine de la Grande-
Bretagne," peroration.
[18] "The Second Coming":
> Turning and turning in the widening gyre
> The falcon cannot hear the falconer;
> Things fall apart; the centre cannot hold;
> Mere anarchy is loosed upon the world. . . .

Anarchy is the state of the kingdom dispossessed of its monarch.
[19] "Hymne to God my God, in my sicknesse":
> I joy, that in these straits, I see my West;
> For, though theire currants yeeld returne to none,
> What shall my West hurt me? As West and East
> In all flatt Maps (and I am one) are one,
> So death doth touch the Resurrection.

With thee
O Let me rise
As larks, harmoniously
And sing this day thy victories:
Then shall the fall further the flight in me.

Thus Vaughan's contemporary, the eagle of Meaux, across the channel wrote:

Après tant de maux at tant de traverses, elle ne connut plus d'autres ennemis que ses péchés. Aucun ne lui sembla léger: elle en faisait un rigoureux examen; et, soigneuse de les expier par le pénitence et par les aumônes, elle était si bien préparée, que la mort n'a pu la surprendre, encore qu'elle soit venue soul l'apparence du sommeil. *Elle est morte, cette grande reine.* Et par sa mort elle a laissé un regret éternel, non seulement à Monsieur et à Madame, qui, fidèles à tous leurs devoirs, ont eu pour elle respects si soumis, si sincères, si persévérants, mais encore à tous ceux qui ont eu l'honneur de la servir ou de la connaître. Ne plaignons plus ses disgrâces, qui font maintenant sa félicité.

"Disgrâces qui font la félicité": the caged-skylark is free,[20] the swan escapes the ice.[21] Death is swallowed up in victory — all by what Hopkins calls simply "the comfort of the Resurrection." And each of these images of Vaughan, Bossuet, Hopkins, Mallarmé is merely glossing the gospel paradox: "Unless the grain of wheat fall into the ground and die, itself remaineth alone." For the priest-poet Vaughan, like the priest-poet Donne, like the priest-poet Bossuet, like the priest-poet Hopkins, indeed like the priest-poet Mallarmé — since every poet, we can now see, is priest — the tragic circle is broken precisely by embracing tragedy (fall into the ground and die to that high requiem) and imping

---

[20] "The Caged Skylark":
    Though aloft on turf or perch or poor low stage,
      Both sing sometimes the sweetest, sweetest spells,
      Yet both droop deadly sometimes in their cells
    Or wring their barriers in bursts of fear or rage.
    Not that the sweet-fowl, song-fowl, needs no rest —
    Why, hear him, hear him babble and drop down to his nest,
      But his own nest, wild nest, no prison.
[21] "La vierge, le vivace et le bel aujourd'hui":
    Tout son col secouera cette blanche agonie
    Par l'éspace infligée à l'oiseau qui le nie,
      Mais non l'horreur du col où le plumage est pris.

man's broken wing to the wing of the phoenix whom the ancient
fathers saw fulfilled in Christ. Only the absolute made concrete
can give the concrete the gift of the absolute. Hence the fascina-
tion of all poets, one thinks immediately of Milton, Hölderlin,
Rilke, Stevens, with the Christian conception of a God-man.
"Christ! What are patterns for?"

The *carmen figuratum*, then, of this notion of salvation is
the cabalistic symbol of the six-pointed star, which Yeats saw
in his own vision of the intersecting spirals, at the mid-point
of which alone — at the very core of the paradox, the *unerhoerte
Mitte* — is redemption attained.[22] It is clear then, the distortion
that was wrought above for pedagogical reasons in not proffering
the whole introduction to the "Morte d'Arthur." For Arthur, as
we know, does not all die; he too shall be resurrected and returned
from Avalon. Hence the complete text, cabalistically we may
now see, moves from the absolute to the contingent and then
out into the absolute again:

> So all day long the noise of battle rolled
> Among the mountains by the winter sea,
> Until King Arthur's table, man by man,
> Had fallen in Lyonnesse about their lord
> King Arthur; then, because his wound was deep,
> The bold Sir Bedivere uplifted him,
> Sir Bedivere, the last of all his knights,
> And bore him to a chapel nigh the field,
> A broken chancel with a broken cross,
> That stood on a dark strait of barren land.
> On one side lay the ocean, and on one
> Lay a great water, and the moon was full.

It is for this salvation that Yeats prayed in a poem which
begins with the same tragic pattern we have encountered earlier:

> Once more the storm is howling, and half hid
> Under this cradle-hood and coverlid
> My child sleeps on.

The evolution is identical. But this is a "prayer for my daughter,"
a supplication that the infinite will not crush the finite, and as

---

22 "Sonette an Orpheus," II, xxviii:
               Du wusstest noch die Stelle, wo die Leier
               sich toenend hob: die unerhoerte Mitte.

such the structure progresses into the linear figure of the resurrection texts above:

> Once more the storm is howling, and half hid
> Under this cradle-hood and coverlid
> My child sleeps on. There is no obstacle
> But Gregory's wood and one bare hill
> Whereby the haystack and roof-levelling wind,
> Bred on the Atlantic, can be stayed;
> And for an hour I have walked and prayed
> Because of the great gloom that is in my mind.
>
> I have walked and prayed for this young child an hour
> And heard the sea-wind scream upon the tower,
> And under the arches of the bridge, and scream
> In the elms above the flooded stream;
> Imagining in excited reverie
> That the future years had come,
> Dancing to a frenzied drum,
> Out of the murderous innocence of the sea.

There is less naïveté here than in Vaughan, and perhaps by that fact less faith in the power of the prayer: the pattern is imposed sonically and thematically rather than pictorially. But it is the same pattern, and all the more clearly so by the repetition of the everyday, commonplace, temporal setting, "I have walked and prayed," at the end of the first and the beginning of the second stanza. The movement is from howling storm, roof-levelling wind, etc., to the slight pedestrian scene of a father thinking about his cradled infant, and then out again to the screaming wind and frenzied drum. (In a different arrangement, "Frost at Midnight," Coleridge introduces all these same components.)

If even the most fragile infant can stand before the great universal storm and not be utterly engulfed, or if engulfed, yet saved, then man is not entirely isolate in the universe.

> Ist nicht so, gejagt und dann gebaendigt,
> diese sehnige Natur des Seins?
> Weg und Wendung. Doch ein Druck verstaendigt.
> Neue Weite. Und *die zwei sind eins*.[23]

As Yeats and Rilke both suggest, there is some reason, or if not reason, some instinct for hope; otherwise, "Wherefore those

---

[23] "Sonette an Orpheus," I, xi.

prayers to the moon?"[24] Man is, and can say, "I am": sum.
But he knows himself to be more than merely this unsponsored
ego; he is a duality destined "to be one." He is therefore a
"sursum," an "I am" that overflows beyond its limns, beyond its
limbs that limit him. The witness of Keats is probative here, both
in the great odes and the two Hyperions. But we must be concerned not with what the poet says but with the framing of his
saws. If man is characterized in Marcel's terms as a sursum,
this quality of breaking out of the imprisoned self to something
transcendent must somehow be expressed in those lines that
most move us. And it is.

I take a passage from a poet now much outmoded by our
minicritics; the poem is "Dining-Room Tea" by Rupert Brooke.
The theme is the poet's glimpse of something timeless in the
most quotidian event. Here is neither the unsoldered fellowship
of Arthur's passing nor the desperate fellowship of "Sunday
Morning"; it has a less portentous ambiance than that. It is as
banal as that of a man musing in a thunderstorm over his sleep-
ing child — and by the fact, "musing upon the king my brother's
wreck."[25] Friends are gathered in careless security when:

> . . . suddenly, and otherwhence,
> I looked on your magnificence.
> I saw the stillness and the light,
> And you august, immortal, white,
> Holy and strange.

The prevalent line is what used to be called "end-stopped," and
the operative device is what used to be called "enjambement."
Each repeated line marches steadily to its terminus, which is
stressed, and breaks against it. The limns are experienced. But
the pattern suddenly is cracked by the absolute necessity of
unstressing "white" and letting the speech flow over (sursum)

---

[24] Stevens, "Annual Gaiety."
[25] Eliot, "The Waste Land":
> A rat crept softly through the vegetation
> Dragging its slimy belly on the bank
> While I was fishing in the dull canal
> On a winter evening round behind the gashouse
> Musing upon the king my brother's wreck
> And on the king my father's death before him.

immediately to the stressed, "Hōly and strange." Again, it is transcendence to which man is missioned; and we now know it because in its analogues — as here — we find peace.

Similarly, in a minor exercise in metaphysical wit called "Dust," Brooke relentlessly stops each of six stanzas with a stressed masculine only to break step in stanza seven with a feminine ending that arabesques immediately into stanza eight. (Stanza six typifies the organization of all the preceding stanzas and is presented here only in illustration of the overall pattern which is about to be violated as two earthly lovers feel the presence of the immortal dead lovers who have been coursing through the universe in search of one another.):

> Nor ever rest, nor ever lie,
> > Till beyond thinking, out of view.
> One mote of all the dust that's I
> > Shall meet one atom that was you.
>
> Then in some garden hushed from wind,
> > Warm in a sunset's afterglow
> The lovers in the flowers will find
> > A sweet and strange unquiet grow
>
> Upon the peace.

Sursum is surprise; that something should break out of its limits shocks and delights (for reasons that should need no repetition now), as in the startling ending to Stevens' "Snow and Stars":

> Let him remove it to his regions,
> White and star-furred for his legions,
> And make much bing, high bing.
>
> It would be ransom for the willow
> And fill the hill and fill it full
> Of ding, ding, dong.

"Could you have said the bluejay suddenly / Would swoop to earth?"[26] Who could have expected that we would conclude on a dissonant instead of the traditionary and riming "ding, dong, ding"? Man is the being that violates patterns: "l'homme passe infiniment l'homme."

A theory of enjambement, then, is a theory of human transcendence, and when we join that conclusion with what we have

---

[26] Stevens, "The Sense of the Sleight-of-hand Man."

already noted of tragedy we have an inkling of why we can
date Shakespeare's plays from the number of so-called "run-on"
lines. The early plays in the old conventional jargon were
"tragedies of fate" and end-stopped lines predominated. In the
tragedy of fate there is no transcendence because there is no
duality at all; the universe is a monadic totality in which genuine
contingency is nonexistent. (From the reverse viewpoint that
is how we have defined comedy.) Transcendence implies dualism,
implies a transitus from *here* to *there*. In a play such as "Romeo
and Juliet," there is no here, all is absorbed by the *there*, by
what could be called the "absolute" — taking the word to mean
an undifferentiated whole. Tragedy of fate takes place in a "pan-
jandrum" cosmos where individuality, particularity, concretion
are insignificant, in fact, are nonexistent because utterly subsumed in the "all." For this reason our sensibilities are not
engaged and there is none of the stark evocation of sympathetic
"pity and fear" we experience, say, with Lear. "Romeo and
Juliet" tells a doleful tale, but it is too ordered, too absolutized
for one to feel anything but a bystander's curiosity at the plight
of the star-crossed (meaning monadized) lovers.

There is no genuine struggle in the tragedy of fate because
struggle says duality, says basically a conflict beween the particular and the forces of the universal. But obviously the particular
cannot collide with the universal unless this universal is experienced. Such experience we have termed a "sense of transcendence"; and the verbal strategy for expressing such a sense
we have termed "enjambement." Rightly did older critics regard
"Julius Caesar" as a crucial hinge-play — though we would
hardly now view it as a cardinal work in the canon — because
in it the man of the absolutely objective ("for always I am
Caesar") is coping not with the "elements" as such, but with
the elements (*read* "particularities") personified in the totally
relative and subjective (Brutus: "I turn the trouble of my
countenance / Merely upon myself"). (Thus the percentage of
run-on lines in "Julius Caesar" is nineteen, compared on the
one hand to thirteen and fourteen for "Richard III" and "Romeo
and Juliet," and on the other hand, twenty-nine and thirty-seven
for "King Lear" and "Macbeth.") If to this it be rejoined that
really all that is happening in the evolution of Shakespeare's

art is his cultivation of a more fluid line, a more conversational
tone, a more true-to-life speech, one can only say: exactly. Conversational tone, true-to-life speech is by definition the speech
of contingency and relativity.

To summarize briefly, before moving to a conclusion: the
infinite is at once the enemy and the mate of the finite, the
tremendum and the fascinosum of theologians, and the "gallant
foe" and the "goodly fere" of poets. The infinite is the central
poem man at once hates and loves, hates because it is perfection which he is not, and loves because perfection is what the
imperfect must aspire to. So too with man, the paradigmatic
poem of the central poem, and with that further reduction from
man, the poem the poet writes: each is the object of a loving
hatred. Says Jeffers: "I hate my verses, every line, every word /
. . . Does it matter whether you hate your . . . self? At least /
Love your eyes that can see, your mind that can / Hear the
music. . . ."

But we must not pause too long over the testimony of poetry;
it is with its framing we have to contend. And the thesis has
been that every poetic construct that moves man does so because it jibes with what he is, because he can lie down (re-latere)
in comfort with it: "la nuance est la seule fiance." The poet
therefore conjoins male and female endings, male and female
words, concretions ("Masculine will only be / Something you
can touch and see") and abstractions ("Nouns ending in -io /
Always a woman show"), particularities and universalities.

This leads into a final exemplum. In a characteristically deft
essay, John Crowe Ransom discussed how the English poet
achieves his finest effects by combining his latin and anglo-
saxon verbal heritage.[27] Ransom analyzed Shakespeare's language
and mined everybody's favorite loci in the plays for their most
attractive hybrids: "absent thee from felicity," "multitudinous
seas," "pendant boughs and coronet weeds" — though, oddly, not
"pendant cradle and procreant bed." But true to his assumed
modesty as major-minor writer, at once affectionate and dis-
missive toward his subject, Ransom didn't bother supplying reasons for everyone's liking this juxtaposition of inflated latinity

---

[27] "On Shakespeare's Language," *Sewanee Review* (Spring, 1947).

and spare anglicism. But it is apparent what those reasons are: the Latin-Anglo-Saxon collision is engaging because the two traditions are polar: polysyllabic-monosyllabic, concrete-abstract, ordinary-exotic, etc., and their fusion sets up once again that basic ontological stance which posits man as the infinite-finite, the transcendent-immanent.

These collisions are not mere embellishments; they are the substance of poetry. And Elder Olson could not have been more wrong when he affirmed: "Shakespeare's profoundest touches are . . . profound, not as meaningful verbal expressions but as actions permitting an extraordinary number of implications, in that they are revelatory of many aspects of character and situation."[28] Nego: character and situation are but other analogues, and in fact more prosaic analogues, of the prime analogate: the limned-unlimited. "The multitudinous seas incarnadine / Making the green one red" says nothing of character and situation, unless we think the murderous queen is Euphues (translate, via Arnold: "sweetness and light"). What such lines do say is that men are defined as the "heavenly labials in a world of gutturals." Why *should* Lady Macbeth talk that way, and why should anyone like this pyrotechnic tour de force's getting in the way of what one is supposed to be really after: "action and character, which cannot be handled in grammatical terms"? (Olson again.)

Of course, such collisions can have a dramatic function, as in de La Mare's "Sam" — who is the Old Testament Samuel listening to the voice of another world:

> Calling me, 'Sam!' — quietlike — 'Sam!' . . .
>   But me . . . I never went,
> Making believe I kind of thought
>   'Twas someone else she meant . . .
> Wonderful lovely there she sat,
>   Singing the night away,
> All in the solitudinous sea
>   Of that there lonely bay.

The collision between the most pretentious latinity ("solitudinous") and the most vulgar colloquialism ("that there") is operative in terms of character and situation: it points up the conflict between the imaginative insight of Sam's childhood and

---

[28] In *Critics and Criticism*, ed. R. S. Crane (Chicago, 1952), pp. 54–55.

the pragmatic cerebration of his old age — though here, too, the dramatic action is merely the "lesser poem" of that "central poem" we have been assaying throughout all of the preceding discussion. Anglo-saxon and latin merge dramatically — but again, it should not be necessary to repeat, derivative of the larger configuration — in Sassoon's "Prehistoric Burials":

> These barrows of the century-darkened dead, —
> Memorials of oblivion, these turfed tombs
> Of muttering ancestries . . .

Here the polarization is of primitive man with his allegedly simple animism and modern self-reflecting man with his ratiocinative inwardness. But — like Shakespeare — that poet whom Sassoon is unwittingly following across Salisbury Plain (*The Prelude*, XIII, 313 ff.) employs these linguistic collisions for their essentially poetic, i.e., ontological effect:[29]

> Redoubled and redoubled, concourse wild
> Of jocund din

This is not fatuous exuberance, decorative verse, the kind of excrescence a "purer" poet would have lopped off. It is the voice of the bard. And it stems explicitly from the entrance of the infinite into the finite:

> . . . and that *uncertain* heaven, received
> Into the bosom of the *steady* lake.

"Uncertain," because man is never really convinced of the reality of the absolute until it enters into his stable, concrete, "steady" contingency. Had we heard these lines running wild in the deserts of Arabia, we would have screamed out in recognition — of ourselves.

So it is with the whole of the tradition. Our "style" is neither attic nor asiatic, neither senecan nor ciceronian, neither concrete nor abstract. It is both. And even in prose we delight at reading: "To be knaved out of our graves, to have our sculs made drinking bowls, and our bones turned into Pipes to delight and sport our Enemies, are Tragical abominations escaped in burning burials." Or, "Tread softly and circumspectly in this funambula-

---

29 *The Prelude*, V, 378–379; 387–388.

tory Track and narrow Path of Goodness."[30] The joy of this comes in no way from the information it provides, which is otiose, nor from the morality it proclaims, which is hackneyed, but from its conformity somehow with what man recognizes himself as being.

The critic's job is not to tell what he likes: that is no cleaner an orthodoxy than to write prose paraphrases of presumably obscure verses. His job is to tell us why what we like *is* like-able. For this reason a theory of poetry is a theory of man, a poetic is a metaphysic, and good poetry is morality.

---

[30] Sir Thomas Browne, *Hydriotaphia*, chapter iii; *Christian Morals*, I, i.

XIII

MATTER ECCLESIA

Within the whole gamut of mental activity there is probably no intellectual discipline flourishing today which, like theology, is so patient of hogwash. The flood of capricious talk, of uncontrolled yawling intended to be taken as serious religious speculation is without abatement. Unchecked flows the swill, and every journalist, licensed by nothing more than baptism and pique, adds his bucket of sludge to the common stream of pure pollution round these human shores. One wouldn't mind if this cloacal tide were merely propaganda in an endless lay-cleric, ancient-modern querelle — the eternal replication on Tiber's banks. One wouldn't mind if the effluvia were compounded merely of high-blown poetic rhetoric — some figures for Scamander. But this turbid flood of anti-God, anti-religion, anti-Church puling does not want to be viewed as propaganda or poetry; it wants to pass as theological discourse — as the very Jordan of salvation.

One cannot therefore dismiss as the result of lyric fancy or polemic grandstanding an assertion like, "Roman Catholicism imposes as a condition for membership belief in its social structure as of divine institution." Nor can one dismiss on those grounds a statement like the following: "Perhaps this is only to say that man's greatness ultimately lies in his ability to resist all spiritualizing tendencies, his willingness (all too infrequent, but increasingly) to refuse belief in a power or a presence which entirely escapes his testing — and, yes, his bounding and naming and understanding." This is not intended to be either poetry or ecclesiastico-political riposte. It is intended to be serious theology.

The first passage is from Charles Davis' *A Question of Conscience*;[1] the second is from Daniel Callahan's defense of Davis,[2] about a third of which was devoted to a selective paraphrase of

---

[1] Cf., *supra*, p. 60.
[2] *Commonweal*, March 29, 1968.

my observations on *A Question of Conscience* in Chapter IV above.[3] In those observations it was asserted that one cannot imagine *any* theologian sustaining Davis' view that, "Roman Catholicism imposes as a condition for membership belief in its social structure . . . ," etc. To which assertion Callahan replied: "What Lawler has done is flatly to deny that anyone of good theological sense holds that Catholicism requires a belief in papacy and hierarchy (which is, after all, what Davis and most other people mean by the Church's 'social structure'). This is an audacious stroke, totally shifting the Catholic reality from where most people, including the bishops and pope, think it is to somewhere else." (There is a syntactic clumsiness about this construction — "after all" — which it would be interesting to analyze, but which is suggestive of a more grievous ham-handed logic, on which, for reasons of space, we must concentrate.)

One is startled immediately in the above passage by the leap away *from* what theology says about the nature of the Church and *to* what "most people" opine its nature to be. As is usual with this ploy there is no indication as to how we know "most people" believe *this*, or even as to whether such people exist. We do know Mr. Callahan believes *this*, and we know, too, he has a penchant for raising autobiography to sociological status, and even, as in this instance, for imposing private views on "bishops and pope." The roseate democratic aura of polling the majority is really, then, masquerade for autocratic ipse dixit. Since factually Mr. Callahan's statement can be proven wrong, and logically it can be proven self-contradictory, all of this is very distressing: because while we may not mind ambiguous overstatement in a propagandist, nor oxymoron in a poet, we have a right to demand verbal and logical rigor in a soi-disant theological writer. First, the fact; then, the illogic.

I quote a distinguished author:

The Church is something of a monarchy since its unique head is Christ, and since the first of its human pastors was the bishop of Rome. It is something of an oligarchy if one considers the small number of those who exercise power in it. It is also something of a democracy by the royal priesthood of the faithful and the apostolic mission which is confided to all its members. But strictly speaking it

---

[3] Pp. 56–61; originally in *Continuum*, Autumn, 1967; and *The Christian Century*, November 22, 1967.

is nothing of each of these in particular and it is something of all of these at once. Christ wished for a minimum of constitutional structure around which the Church has developed its organization according to extremely variable forms depending on people, times, and places. This diversity of its contingent nature is able to evolve indefinitely, while preserving the intangible core of the constitution willed by its divine founder.[4]

Apparently, then, what is of divine institution is not the Church's contingent nature but its "intangible core," a core which not even Mr. Callahan's fiats can make equatable with "pope and bishops." (One regrets having to point out that the words above are the words of one of those very bishops so casually numbered by Mr. Callahan among those "most people" who are in unanimity with him — and all of whom, presumably, Mr. Callahan has queried, consulted, and polled on their beliefs.) Second, as to the self-defeating logic of Mr. Callahan's neat collection of surds, the really "audacious shift" is his from (1) "a divinely instituted social structure" (a contradiction in terms since by definition *all* divine institution is of the absolute and *all* social structure is of the relative — but let it pass), to (2) "papacy and hierarchy," to (3) "the Catholic reality." Thus are conflated social structure, popes and bishops, and *the* Catholic reality: a conflation which allows no place whatever to Mr. Callahan's own office (Mind of the Catholic Layman, wasn't it?) and no place to those "most people" whose activities and opinions are, otherwise, so compelling.

Having rhetorically painted himself into this corner, Mr. Callahan can do nothing other than defend his position. The stance is heroic, evoking Farinata cursing the absolute, Orlando furioso staving off the Saracens of duality: the social structure *is* the reality, the embodiment *is* the embodied, and ultimately, as we have seen from the longer quotation with which we began, for Mr. Callahan, the matter *is* the spirit.

First we will look at why anyone *might want to appear as though* he believed this, and second we will look at the *this* itself.

I take it that what makes man a being worthy of respect is his willingness to "historify" and "objectivize" his visions, to refuse to render them incapable of testing, to refuse to settle for a "spiritual" reality at the expense of an "objective" reality. Perhaps this is only to say that man's greatness ultimately lies in his ability to resist all spiritualiz-

---

[4] Maximos IV, *L'Eglise grecque melkite au Concile* (Beirut, 1967), p. 171.

ing tendencies, his willingness (all too infrequent, but increasing) to
refuse belief in a power or a presence which entirely escapes his testing
— and, yes, his bounding and naming and understanding.

Phrased still another way, would it not be worth exploring the
possibility that faith in the spirit has been allowed to overshadow
the great human meaning of the incarnation? That meaning is that
God foreswore all images of transcendent, incalculable spirit for the
sake of an objective, testable body; and, beyond that, an objective,
testable Church. For once, in the Christian belief in the incarnation,
man had the courage to repudiate "imageless voids" and immaterial,
"spiritual" gods; he staked himself on a person in a body, who had a
name. . . . We are in our own hands, and in the figure of the bodily,
all-too-human Jesus we have a consummate exemplar of what it means
to be a materialistic believer and to exist in a supremely bodily community, one which, when it discovered the failure of its infinite hopes,
set about creating finite ones. If there is a final Christian sanity,
there it lies.

It is a brave speech the doughty warrior has delivered (heart-
stirring even, one might have said in a more dualistic age.) Who
so thick skinned as to be untouched by this sturdy, blunt talk? We
shall go down faithful to our pledged humanity, defending our
earthly realm, our spouse and folk, our oaten bread and kind, here
at this Hastings of the spirit — or rather, of the body; and woe
to the mercenaries of *logos turannos* who land on these our shores.

Too bad we have heard it all before, in accents ignoble and of
pedigree debased. The voice indeed is the voice of peace and
freedom and openness, but the hands, "our own hands," are literally
the hands of the manipulator, of the button-pusher. It is the
Faustian speech of totalism, of the great monad where the unpredictable, the untestable are prohibited, where the bells of St.
Clement never sound, where ultimately, the secular city is placed
in direct line with Pandemonium and Belsen. For, without a belief
in the utterly untestable, in the utterly unmeasurable, in the un-
bound and unnamed and un-understandable, man is prey to all
the feral, fatal instincts it has taken centuries of the effluence of
spirit to channel.

Now, no one denies that the very notion of "spirit," or "other
world," of "immortality," of "infinity" has been abused and
subverted to venal ends, to what Mr. Callahan brightly calls
"pie-in-the-sky theology." Yet no abuses ought to lead us to
abandon so readily the habit of nice discrimination. The corrective

of pie-in-the-sky theology is not mud-pie theology, it is simply
theology. It is more than that, however, it is that whole realm of
the untestable, unbounded, unnamed, etc., that whole realm which
poets and people who pray and love inhabit. Mr. Callahan sees
pie in the sky. There are those who have seen something else.

> . . . I lift up heart, eyes,
> Down all that glory in the heavens to glean our Savior.[5]

Mr. Callahan, having so publicly exercised his muddy herme-
neutic on the scriptures in the above long quotation, allows us to
inquire as to how accurate is his exegesis. Of course, in a certain
sense, we are in our own hands; in a certain sense, the body is
the spirit; in a certain sense, the intellect is everything. But all is
dependent on that "in a certain sense" — which brings us to the
core of the whole tradition of the paradox of transcendence-
immanence, spirit-matter, infinite-finite, etc. — all of which Mr.
Callahan seems not to know exists. In the old language — which is
as good as any — of premotio physica, the mystery remains that
God moves free beings freely, so that while we are in our hands,
in a much deeper sense we are only in God's hands, along with
the whole wide world. This is the lesson that the "all too human"
Jesus taught when he commended himself into the hands of the
Father. Nor did the "supremely bodily" Jesus raise his body from
the dead: it "was raised from the dead" — or are those scriptures
also to be rejected because they escape our testing or affront our
"human dignity, reason and power"?

We have seen why it is that someone would want to appear as
though he believed spirit is matter — it is the old Promethean
itch; we have not yet seen what it means to believe this. First we
must look at Mr. Callahan's views, and then — if one may be
allowed the expression — at some metaphysics. The physics runs
like this: "For once, in the Christian belief in the incarnation,
man had the courage to repudiate 'imageless voids' and immaterial, 'spiritual' gods; he staked himself on a person, in a body,
who had a name." Then follows, in reply to my censure of Davis
for his materialism, Callahan's exclamation: "Would that this were
true." Apparently, then, Mr. Callahan does think that he thinks
spirit to be matter, or rather that matter is all. And hence only

---

[5] G. M. Hopkins, "Hurrahing in Havest."

that ecclesiology will be truly "magnificent" which is "systematically materialistic." To this end we must reject all "infinite hopes" and create "finite ones"; like the God Mr. Callahan worships, we are to foreswear "all images of transcendent, incalculable spirit for the sake of an objective, testable body." This is the program: a thoroughgoing, unblushing materialism culminating in the building of the heavenly Jerusalem in this green and pleasant land.

But is Mr. Callahan *really* a materialist? Does he really subscribe to his own rhetoric, or is he perhaps merely the victim of his own penchant for over-stating and over-reacting, the victim, in short, of a *ressentiment* which panders to his "instinct to go to the jugular vein of the institutional Church" — an instinct which he seems to think universal and normal, but which may as well be idiosyncratic and pathological. How ingrained is this materialism? Mr. Callahan writes as though he were a true minister at the shrine of all-encompassing matter. He has publicly renewed his vows to this *totum* totem on any number of occasions, most notably when commenting on Chapter I above, "Theology and the Uses of History," a comment which concluded to the non-reality of the transcendent, or at least to its non-reality for Mr. Callahan.[6]

But does he really believe his own words? Does he not, at least occasionally, break out of the closed monad and postulate, and ultimately affirm, another principle than matter? May it not be that it is only a latent and unformulated belief in spirit — and hence a failure in self-reflection — that allows him to opt so utterly for matter as the total omnium? Mr. Callahan has written: "If my wife was suddenly arrested for murder, arson, dope peddling and a series of bank robberies, I would undoubtedly deny (for I love her) that these acts have anything to do with her reality, which only I am privileged to know. And my faith in her would probably be excused, though not adopted, by others. Similarly, I suppose we should be ready to forgive those who so love the Church that they are prepared to discern — with the eye of faith — some hidden experiential data which they label the reality." Presumably then loving a person is more than merely a question of body dynamics, of contiguity, tangibility, and plumbing. But what is this "more than"? Will it satisfy Mr. Callahan's brave

---

[6] *Commonweal*, August 19, 1966.

demand that it be "objective, testable"? And if this "more than" is *entirely* materialistic (for it is a question of a complete materialism, not a sham one whereby we loudly vaunt matter while furtively dissembling our dependence on spirit) what are the instruments, what are the techniques, what are the methods, for testing this "totally objective" reality? How heavy is that reality? What are its precise dimensions, at what point does it begin and at what point does it stop, for begin and stop it must, since all infinity has been ruled out?

Again, we are told in pursuit of our "systematic materialism" that at the time of the incarnation of Christ, man "staked himself on a person, in a body, who had a name." Indeed. But we are staking ourselves "on a person *in a body*"; hardly a very systematic materialism after all: in fact as dualistic as the crudest hylomorphism. Within this body, on Mr. Callahan's own word, there is something called "person," which must therefore be *other* than body, else why any distinction at all? Now, as everybody for two and a half millenia has recognized, "spirit" may not be the best name for that "other," for that non-measurable, non-testable reality; let us call it "interiority," "the within," "core of being" or, translate the latter literally and, call it the "heart" or, with the poet seek to express the withinness of the withinness of the withinness, etc. — since it is a question of infinity — and call it the "deep heart's core." Obviously all names for this must be inadequate. The infinite *is* the indefinable.

Now for the small lesson in metaphysics promised earlier: embarrassing to write, and above all embarrassing to have to read, since Mr. Callahan certainly long ago must have learned it well, perhaps had even learned it "by heart." Let us assume that Mr. Callahan's program is viable, that there is nothing that "escapes man's testing," that we must foreswear "all images of transcendent, incalculable spirit for the sake of an objective, testable body." Let us assume all this. We must then ask, how shall we test? But even prior to this we shall have to ask, what is a "test" itself. Perhaps, we look to the etymology and learn that the word means a shell, a casing, a coating, a container; this won't help our program much because our basic premise is that the container *is* the contained, or more traditionally, the matter is the spirit (matter = metre = measure). But if the two are utterly identical (that's what "is" means) we cannot compare "one" with "another"; we do not even have "one" and "another."

Well, let us abandon etymology. From Cratylus through Aquinas those versed in the tradition like Mr. Callahan have known what pitfalls imperil wanderers through that thicket, that loom of language. Away, then, with this web of Webster — "The silken weavings of our afternoons" — and let us, perhaps somewhat desperately, take a universal definition of "test," one rigorously applicable to our author's commitment to "bounding and naming and understanding." The dictionary provides: "a). that with which anything is compared for proof of genuineness; b). a procedure or reaction used to distinguish any particular substance or constituent." The operative words remain "compare" and "distinguish" and again our "systematic materialism" is stymied by the refractoriness of reality, because both "compare" and "distinguish" demand an alterity, a *something* and a *something else* which differs from it. The ultimate principle is simply that all meaning requires a duality.

How distressing that such truisms must be enunciated to philosophers by mere professors of poetry, but this is not the first time the infima doctrina has illuminated sacra doctrina, nor shall it be the last. As to the relation of all this to ecclesiology proper, when Mr. Callahan takes another header into the higher pantheism it will be a pleasure to apply this well-worn doctrine to that institutional Church whose jugular Mr. Callahan makes his living by fondling. For now, it is enough to note — as was noted in detail in the original *Continuum* piece on Davis — that if we are staking ourselves "on a person, in a body," we necessarily are staking ourselves on the inevitable polarities in all reality, on the fact that "personhood" — whatever that is precisely — is always both concealed and disclosed by "embodiment" — whatever that is precisely.

By definition the institutional Church can never be the perfect expression of Christ; the institutional Church, like every body, is the sign that obscures as it clarifies. That perfect expression can only be in the sacraments, the single reality in which spirit is matter, in which the outward sign *is* the inward grace. The institutional Church, then, is not the primal sacrament: the primal sacrament is the God-man, not as Callahan would have it with a self-contradictory lucretian cartesianism, "a God, in a man" (Cf. "a person, in a body"), but simply the God-man, the being who has entirely "come home to himself." A whole theology could be written on "the hyphenating Christ," in fact it has been written. Though it may bother our anti-episcopal railers, we must be clear that that theology is nothing other than a theology of the bishop's office, a theology of the pontiff who bridges the gap by following in the footsteps of the "one mediator" who has definitively put together the divided image, whose sacraments in this world are the foretaste and pledge of that final self-reunion we shall know in another "world."

A last note. Mr. Callahan closes by citing Harvey Cox who "once wrote somewhere that the coming struggle in the Church would be between the religious and the non-religious Christian. It is about time that this struggle started taking place." The real struggle predates Christianity; it is between totalitarian Apollo, lord of the measuring rod, and volatile Hermes. Since that kind of obsolete imagery means nothing to our ultra-contemporary theological journalists, we might want to see the struggle between the Coleridgeans and Benthamites, or, in less secular terms, between the Newmans and the Pio Nonos. And let us not be misled by labels: the measurers, the testers, the definers are all in one camp, whether they be definers of God like Callahan or definers of dogma like Pius IX. That camp is the camp of the well-intentioned Grand Inquisitor who hating the unpredictable, and having "discovered the failure of infinite hopes set about creating finite ones."

I close this chapter and this book with a poem by Stevens and a suitably brief *explication de texte*.

> To what good, in the alleys of the lilacs,
> O caliper, do you scratch your buttocks
> And tell the divine ingénue, your companion,
> That this bloom is the bloom of soap
> And this fragrance the fragrance of vegetal?
> Do you suppose that she cares a tick,
> In this hymeneal air, what it is
> That marries her innocence thus,
> So that her nakedness is near,
> Or that she will pause at scurrilous words?
> Poor buffo! Look at the lavender

> And look your last and look still steadily,
> And say how it comes that you see
> Nothing but trash and that you no longer feel
> Her body quivering in the Floreal
> Toward the cool night and its fantastic star,
> Prime paramour and belted paragon,
> Well-booted, rugged, arrogantly male,
> Patron and imager of the gold Don John,
> Who will embrace her before summer comes.[7]

"Caliper" is the systematic materialist; the "divine ingénue" is being in this world; "fragrance" is the epiphany of that being; the "prime paramour" is being itself, the Logos; "summer" is the final summation and consummation.

All poems are one poem. It is time we began to learn them and it.

---

[7] "Last Look at the Lilacs."

INDEX